Family Child Care

Business Planning Guide

Being a Family Child Care Professional

Family child care is a special profession for those who love young children. As a professional family child care provider, you must balance the skills required to care for children with those required to operate your business. Here are some tips to help you do this:

- Learn the child care regulations for your area, and follow them.
- Join your local family child care association.
- Sign up with your local child care resource and referral agency.
- Join the Child and Adult Care Food Program (CACFP).
- Find good professional advisors (such as a tax professional, insurance agent, and lawyer).
- Actively participate in training to acquire and improve your professional skills.

Additional Resources

Redleaf Press and Resources for Child Caring are two leading organizations that share the goal of helping your family child care business succeed. Resources for Child Caring (www .resourcesforchildcare.org) can answer your business questions; its Web site is filled with free handouts, articles, and newsletters. Redleaf Press (www.redleafpress.org; 800-423-8309) publishes resources for family child care. We offer the following publications to support your business. For more information, see www.redleafpress.org.

- Starting a family child care business:
  Family Child Care Business Planning Guide

- Promoting your business:
  Family Child Care Marketing Guide

- Creating contracts and policies:
  Family Child Care Contracts and Policies, 3rd Edition
  Redleaf Complete Forms Kit for Family Child Care Providers

- Keeping accurate records and filing your taxes:
  Family Child Care Record-Keeping Guide, 8th Edition
  The Redleaf Calendar-Keeper: A Record-Keeping System for Family Child Care Professionals
  Family Child Care Tax Workbook and Organizer
  Family Child Care Tax Companion

- Reducing business risks:
  Family Child Care Legal and Insurance Guide

- Managing your money and planning for retirement:
  Family Child Care Money Management and Retirement Guide

Family Child Care

Business Planning Guide

Tom Copeland, JD

Redleaf Press®
www.redleafpress.org
800-423-8309

Published by Redleaf Press
10 Yorkton Court
St. Paul, MN 55117
www.redleafpress.org

Printed in the United States of America

18 17 16 15 14 13 12 11   2 3 4 5 6 7 8 9

Library of Congress Cataloging-in-Publication Data
Copeland, Tom.
   Family child care business planning guide / Tom Copeland.
      p. cm.
   ISBN 978-1-60554-008-5
   1. Family day care—United States. 2. Family day care—United States—Management
3. Family day care—United States—Finance.   I. Title.
HQ778.63.C649 2008
362.71'2068—dc22
                                                      2008033979

FSC
Mixed Sources
Product group from well-managed
forests and other controlled sources

Cert no. SW-COC-002283
www.fsc.org
© 1996 Forest Stewardship Council

Disclaimer

Redleaf Press and the author are not engaged in rendering legal, accounting, or financial advice or any other
professional services, and we are not responsible for the outcome of how the information in this book is
interpreted or applied. Readers who want professional advice about their money or investments should consult a qualified, experienced financial advisor.

Printed on acid-free paper

Contents

Acknowledgments

Many people have contributed to this book, including thousands of family child care providers who have shared their stories in my training sessions over the past 26 years and over 500 providers who responded to the online money management survey discussed in this book. Thanks to all of them.

Thanks also to the following people, who reviewed this book and offered valuable suggestions that made it better:

- Tax and financial planning professionals: Benjamin Cohen, Barbara Delbene, Tom Jemison, Shaun McHale, Jeff Robinson, Sandy Schroeder, Al Wroblewski, and Pinghau Yin.

- Family child care providers: Olga Anderson, Sarah Beck, Kalissa Braga, Laurie De Martini, Pat Goor, Traci Heilman, Roxanne Johnson, Patty Kelly, Bonna Lake, Patricia Lee, Debbie Moore, Linda Powell, Tiffany Sartin, Pamela Schmitz, Loretta Spindler, Lorna Tall, Michelle Thole, and Reva Wywadis.

Others who have contributed to this book include Jan Stokley, Diane Copeland, Kathy Modigliani, and Paul Bloomer. Thanks to David Heath for project management; Laurie Herrmann, Carla Valadez, Douglas Schmitz, and Jim Handrigan for production assistance; and Jan Grover and Beth Wright for proofreading.

I want to give special thanks to my editor, Rose Brandt. Rose has been my editor for seven previous books, and her work has greatly contributed to their success. She is a painstakingly thorough editor who has improved the clarity of all my books. Her work on this book is especially noteworthy, and her numerous suggestions have improved every section. I cannot thank her enough for many years of excellent work.

How This Book Can Help You

Chapter Summary
This chapter explains how business planning can help you manage your
family child care business more effectively, whether you have an ongoing
business or are thinking of opening a new family child care business.

Most family child care providers have experience caring for children before they begin
offering care to other families. However, few providers have experience starting and managing their own business. For this reason, over the years many providers have asked me for a
resource that would help them get their business properly organized right from the start.

This book meets that need. It is organized around the resources in the appendixes—two
blank plans that you can fill out to set up your business properly and two financial tools that
you can use to budget and plan your business finances:

- **Start-Up Plan (Appendix A)**. Completing a start-up plan will help you to handle the
  issues that must be addressed before your business begins, identify the costs involved in
  starting your business, and set up the key terms of your contract and policies.

- **Business Plan (Appendix B)**. Completing a business plan will help you to plan how to
  market your business, protect yourself with insurance, set up your program, and keep the
  necessary business records.

- **Financial Tools (Appendix C)**. Preparing a budget and cash flow projection will make
  it easier for you to meet your financial goals, whether you are a new or an experienced
  provider.

This book outlines a clear path that will help you to either get a new business started in a
businesslike way or manage an existing business more effectively. I hope that the information in this book will help you learn new skills so you can enjoy the work you love most—
caring for children. However, this book doesn't include all the resources you'll need to run
a successful family child care business; it's intended to be used with the other books in the
Redleaf Press business series:

- *The Redleaf Calendar-Keeper*
- *Family Child Care Record-Keeping Guide,* 7th Edition
- *Family Child Care Tax Workbook and Organizer*
- *Family Child Care Tax Companion*
- *Family Child Care Contracts and Policies*
- *Family Child Care Marketing Guide*
- *Family Child Care Legal and Insurance Guide*
- *Family Child Care Money Management and Retirement Guide*

The books in this series offer a depth of information that will answer all your questions about operating a family child care business. However, you don't need to read all of these books before you open your business—you'll be ready to go after you complete the plans and budget explained in this book. You can add the other books to your library as needed to help manage your business and make it more successful.

Tax note: This book refers to tax laws that are subject to change. For the latest tax rules and information, consult the current edition of the *Tax Workbook and Organizer*.

• •

A Note about Gender
Studies show that over 95% of family child care providers are female. In this book I will use female pronouns to describe family child care providers and male pronouns to describe their spouses. I've made this choice to avoid the awkward use of "she or he"; however, I don't mean to slight any male family child care providers or female spouses who may be reading this book.

• •

Treat Your Business Like a Business
In 2007 we posted a money management survey on our Web site, and over 500 family child care providers responded. (You can view the results at www.redleafpress.org—enter "Business Planning Guide" into the search field, and follow the links.) The responses showed us that many providers would like to learn how to manage their business more effectively. For example, one experienced provider wrote:

I feel that we older providers—and maybe the younger ones, too—went into this business thinking it was just something to do while our children were young—we didn't really view it as a business at first. We were just so grateful to be at home with our children, and we didn't lay down a solid business plan. When we finally started thinking about how to secure our future, we realized that it would take a lot of courage and drastic changes to the way we do business. Even now, that's one of the most difficult parts of the business for me.

In other words, it's important to "treat your business as a business, rather than a hobby," as another provider told me. A hobby is something that you do just for fun. The work that you do as a family child care provider may be deeply rewarding, but you know that it involves a lot more than just having fun.

One of the most important steps in "treating your business like a business" is preparing a formal business plan—a comprehensive blueprint for how you'll run your business. This book outlines, step by step, how to prepare all the elements of a plan for your business:

- Chapter 1 explains how a business plan can help you and describes the major components of a family child care business plan.

- Chapters 2 and 3 address the planning issues essential to starting (or thinking of starting) a new family child care business. Some of this information may also be helpful for experienced providers.

- Chapter 4 outlines the seven components that should be included in any family child care provider's business plan.

- Chapter 5 explains how to prepare a budget (financial plan) in detail, based on a sample budget that you can use as a template.

- Chapter 6 describes some of the ways that you can use your budget to manage your business finances more effectively.

I suggest that you start by reading the entire book and flagging the information that interests you or that applies to your business. Once you have that overview of the steps involved in the planning process, return either to chapter 2 (for a start-up business) or to chapter 4 or 5 (for an ongoing business) to start working on your plan.

Why Do You Need a Business Plan?

I know that business planning is probably pretty low on your list of favorite activities. It's unlikely that you'll ever turn to your significant other and say, "Sorry, sweetheart, I'm just not in the mood for dinner and dancing tonight—I'd rather stay home and work on my annual budget."

No, preparing a business plan isn't an exciting task, and it may even seem quite intimidating, especially if you've never done anything like this before. However, paying closer attention to your business will have a significant payoff, and the hours you spend on planning may end up being the most important time you spend on your business, other than actually caring for the children.

Planning for a Start-Up Business

Preparing a plan is essential if you are starting a new family child care business, because the plan you prepare may well mean the difference between success and failure for your new enterprise. For example, the planning process for a start-up business plan accomplishes several things:

- Make sure that you satisfy all the legal requirements for providing child care in your state *before* you invest a lot of time and money in setting up your new business. (See the section on legal and regulatory issues in chapter 3.)

- Figure out what your start-up expenses will be and decide how you'll get the money to pay for them. (See the section on start-up costs in chapter 3.)

- Decide in advance how to operate your program and set your policies so you'll be able to respond effectively to problems as they arise, rather than reacting to crises on the spur of the moment. (See the section on contracts and policies in chapter 3.)

- Decide how to promote your business to maximize your chances of success. (See the marketing plan section of chapter 4.)

- Make sure that you start out with all the insurance you need to operate legally and protect yourself from the risks involved in running your business. (See the insurance plan section of chapter 4.)

- Budget to plan ahead for potential financial obstacles so that they don't take you by surprise. (See the financial plan section of chapters 4 and 5.)

Planning for an Ongoing Business

Preparing a business plan is also very useful for an ongoing business, especially if you're trying to establish your operations on a more businesslike basis. The planning process offers several advantages:

- A chance to reevaluate and rethink your program. ("Should I try some new marketing approaches?")

- A financial spring-cleaning. ("Is it time to create a budget to help manage my spending?")

- A review of your practices to clean out anything that's outdated and fill in any gaps. ("Should I overhaul my contract? Should I add more paid vacation time?")

- A review of your insurance policies to ensure you're adequately covered. ("Is it time to increase the coverage limits on my business liability policy?")

- Help in meeting your short-term financial goals. ("What changes would allow me to put more money into an emergency fund? Should I cut back on buying toys? Should I start charging for another federal holiday?")

- Help in meeting your long-term financial goals. ("What changes would let me save more money for retirement? Should I raise my rates? Add another child to my program?")

In addition to the benefits listed above, an up-to-date business plan will also be very helpful if you ever want to apply for a business or personal loan. Your plan will strengthen your loan application by showing your lender that you're handling your business in a professional way. (For more information about managing the financial side of your business, setting short-term and long-term financial goals, and applying for a business loan, see the *Money Management and Retirement Guide*.)

• •

If You Need Help

Most family child care providers will be able to write their own business plan by following the instructions in this book. However, if you feel overwhelmed, aren't sure how to proceed, or just want some help, don't hesitate to ask for assistance.

For example, you can talk to another provider who has already written a business plan. You can ask your local child care resource and referral agency, your local family child care association, or your Food Program sponsor for advice or a referral to someone who can provide more help. If you're working with a tax preparer, attorney, or financial planner, that person may also be able to help you with certain areas of your business plan.

• •

How to Get Your Plan Done

You don't have to prepare all the planning tools described in this book at once. If it seems too daunting to write an entire business plan all at once, start with the first step—read through this book and become familiar with the steps of the planning process. Then set a goal to complete your business plan and take your plan one section at a time. (To make it easier to get started, be sure to use the blank plans provided in the appendixes.)

It may be easiest to start with a topic that you've already given some thought to or have some experience with. For example, if you already have some ideas about your professional development goals, then start by filling in that section. Once that section is done, review another section and jot down any ideas you have about it.

There's no rush; just try to make steady progress and complete another section whenever you can. Before you know it, your plan will be done!

You can also benefit from this book even if you don't have the time to write up a formal business plan right now. For example, you might compare your own practices to the ideas suggested here and see if there are any improvements you'd like to make right away. You may also find some tips that can help you manage your business or save time and money.

What's in a Business Plan?

A complete plan for a family child care business will include the following sections:

- a start-up plan (for new businesses only)
- a statement of your hopes and goals for the business
- a marketing plan
- an insurance plan
- a program plan
- a professional development plan
- a record-keeping plan
- a financial plan (budget)

If you're about to open (or have just opened) a new family child care business, then your business plan should begin with your start-up plan, which I'll explain in chapter 3. The other seven sections listed above are necessary parts of a business plan for any family child care business, new or ongoing. Chapter 4 will guide you in preparing these seven sections, supplemented by the more detailed instructions for preparing a budget in chapter 5.

However, you don't need to prepare your plan in the order listed above. I'd suggest that you start by reading the entire book to get an overview of the planning process. Then proceed as follows:

- If you're planning for a start-up business, begin by weighing the issues discussed in chapter 2. If you decide to proceed, do your start-up plan first (chapter 3) and then either your business plan or your first-year budget (described in chapters 4 and 5, respectively).

- If you're planning for an ongoing business, start working on the seven sections described in chapters 4 and 5, completing them in any order that you wish.

• •

Keep Your Plan Updated

To be most helpful, your business plan should be a living document that evolves as your business changes and you gain experience. I suggest that you review and update your plan periodically—perhaps every year, or whenever there's a change in your personal or business circumstances, such as an addition to your family or a move or expansion of your business. For example, if you move, you'll need to review your insurance policies (see chapter 4) and see if there are any regulatory issues or barriers to doing business at your new address (see chapter 3).

• •

CHAPTER TWO

Is Family Child Care for You?

Chapter Summary

This chapter examines the financial and nonfinancial considerations that you should weigh before deciding to open a new family child care business. It explains what you should know if you're considering offering exempt or illegal care and the tax implications of the expenses for your new business.

If you're considering opening a new family child care business, before you do any start-up planning you should take a good look at the financial realities of your new venture—you'll need to decide whether you really *can* afford to work out of your home. Most people who are considering opening a family child care business aren't doing it for the money. Instead, their reasons include the following:

- I love children.
- I want to work at home so I can be with my children or grandchildren.
- I want to be my own boss.
- I want to make a difference in the lives of young children and help them succeed.
- I want to help support families who have young children.

As one provider in our survey put it, "I don't do this job for the money. I just want to be at home with my children at this stage, and I love the children I care for. I love being able to provide a safe and happy home for all the children in my care."

Although these are all perfectly legitimate reasons for starting a family child care business, child care providers are also increasingly seeking better financial rewards for their work. Furthermore, family child care is not a business for everyone. Too many people jump into this field without considering the financial consequences of their decision. They don't have a realistic idea of how much money they will make, and they aren't able to fill their program as quickly as they thought they could. As a result, they go out of business after six months or a year because they can't pay their bills. Other providers continue to struggle financially, hanging on somehow for a few years—or sometimes, for many years.

The next three chapters will explain how to carefully plan and budget your new business to avoid these kinds of pitfalls. However, before you start that planning process, there are two issues that you should consider: Is this really the right business for me? Can I afford to work at home?

In this chapter, I will help you answer these questions and address two more considerations that you should understand at this early stage—the implications of operating as an exempt or illegal provider and the tax consequences of any remodeling projects and other expenses that you incur in preparation for your new business.

Is This Business for You?

In considering whether to open a family child care business, you've probably thought about all the reasons you want to work in this field. However, before proceeding you should also honestly weigh the potential drawbacks of caring for young children in your home:

- A family child care business requires working very long hours with few breaks and no employer-paid benefits.

- A family child care business in your home affects your entire family; it may inconvenience or interfere with the activities of your spouse or children, creating more stress in your family.

- You may earn less doing family child care than you could earn in another line of work. In addition to lowering your current standard of living, child care may lower the Social Security income you will receive in retirement, as well as how much you're able to save for retirement during your working years.

Finally, consider that operating a successful small business requires you to become a jack of all trades—you'll have to learn a wide range of skills and handle some roles that you may not enjoy as much as caring for children. Running your business will require you to wear many hats:

- Prepare budgets and keep careful records (accountant)
- Promote and market your program (marketer)
- Write and enforce your contracts and policies (lawyer)
- Make sure you're paid on time (bill collector)
- Learn as much as you can about child development (student)
- Manage conflicts with your clients (counselor and mediator)
- Hire and supervise any employees and handle your payroll taxes and forms (human resources and payroll manager)

You may feel ready for a change and view these challenges as exciting opportunities to expand your horizons and develop new skills. Or you may decide that one or more of these considerations could be a deal-breaker in your case. It's up to you. I simply suggest that you seriously consider these issues now, before you make a major commitment to your new career, rather than later, when your options will be more limited.

Can You Afford to Work at Home?

Before you decide to start a new family child care business, it's important to understand the financial trade-offs involved in this decision. Most importantly, I suggest that you compare the take-home pay you can earn working outside your home with the profit you'll be likely to make providing family child care in your home. A realistic comparison of your income and expenses for each option will give you an idea of what to expect financially from your new business.

The worksheets in tables 1 and 2 are designed to help you make this comparison—these worksheets show a filled-in column for a provider named Kally and another blank column for your own numbers.

Bear in mind that the numbers used in the example columns are estimates, and your own situation may be quite different from Kally's. However, these worksheets show that Kally would make substantially more money, for fewer hours of work, by staying in her current job rather than opening a family child care business in her home.

The biggest factor that will influence your business income is the number of children in your care. Since state licensing rules are likely to limit the number and ages of the children you may care for, be sure to check those rules at an early stage in your planning.

In addition, you should think carefully about how many children, and of what ages, you *want* to care for. Although you can earn more caring for infants and toddlers than you can caring for preschoolers, you will be allowed to care for more preschoolers than younger children. (From a financial perspective, another consideration is how many children you *need* to care for to cover your expenses—this calculation is explained in chapter 6.)

When you fill out this worksheet, begin by projecting your income based on the number of children and age groups that you ideally want to care for, bearing in mind the regulations in your state. If caring for this ideal number of children doesn't provide the profit you want, then you might want to consider caring for more (or younger) children. The biggest mistake that most new providers make is expecting to make it financially by caring for only a couple of children.

Although it's important to understand the financial implications of choosing to do family child care, I'm not suggesting that the results of your worksheet should determine your decision. As I mentioned at the start of this chapter, money is often not the primary motivation for going into this business.

Many new providers simply want to work at home so they can care for their own children or other children in their extended family. Others intentionally choose to care for a small number of children to ensure that they will be able to offer high-quality care. In these cases, making more money clearly isn't the most important consideration. However, the more you know about the financial realities of your new business, the better the chances that you'll be able to support yourself by working at home doing something you love.

Table 1. Worksheet: Take-home pay working as a family child care provider

Income			Kally's Numbers	Your Numbers
Goal for number of full-time children in care			6	_____
Average fee per week, per child [a]			$120	_____
Average weekly income (number of children x average weekly fee)			$720	_____
Annual income (50 weeks for Kally) (average weekly income x number of weeks you will work)			$36,000	_____
Food Program reimbursements [b]	Kally	You		
Number of children served on Tier I: ____ x $982 per year	$0	_____		
Number of children served on Tier II: ____ x $473 per year	$2,838	_____		
Total Food Program reimbursements			$2,838	_____
Total business income (annual income + Food Program income)			$38,838	_____
Reduce total income by 20% (to project an 80% enrollment rate)			– $7,768	_____
Adjusted total business income			$31,070	_____

Expenses				
Business expenses (not including home expenses) [c]	Kally	You		
Food ($4 per day per child)	$6,000	_____		
Toys	$1,500	_____		
Supplies	$1,500	_____		
Car expenses	$600	_____		
Helpers	$2,000	_____		
Other	$0	_____		
Other	$0	_____		
Total business expenses [d]			$11,600	_____
Business profit ($31,070 – $11,600)			$19,470	_____
Taxes (30.3% of tentative business profit for Kally) [e]			– $5,899	_____
Health insurance premiums			– $6,000	_____
Retirement contribution after tax deduction ($1,000 – $150 tax deduction)			– $850	_____
Take-home pay working as a family child care provider			$6,721	_____

Table 1 *Notes*

a. For help estimating what you might be able to charge for child care, see chapter 5. In your average fee per child, consider any payments you may receive from a subsidy program, as discussed in that chapter.

b. The Food Program is explained in chapter 3. The reimbursement rates shown here are the 2007–2008 rates, but this is just an example calculation, since these rates will rise every year. (The rates are higher in Alaska and Hawaii.) For the current rates, visit www.resourcesforchildcare.org. (For Kally's numbers, we are using the Tier II rates. All family child care providers are eligible to receive reimbursements at the Tier II rate. If your family is low-income, you serve low-income children, or you live in a low-income area, you will qualify to receive the higher Tier I rate.)

c. We haven't included housing expenses here (rent, utilities, home mortgage interest, or home insurance, repairs, or depreciation), since you'd still have to pay these expenses if you didn't have a child care business. However, as a family child care provider, part of these expenses is deductible, reducing your taxes.

d. It can be very difficult to estimate your business expenses before starting your business; for a shortcut, see chapter 5. This example doesn't include any of the start-up costs discussed in chapter 3.

e. The taxes you'll need to pay depend on your business profit. As of 2007, the federal income tax rates were 10%, 15%, 25%, and 33%. You'll also need to pay 15.3% of your profit for Social Security taxes (unless your profit is less than $400). In Kally's numbers, we're using a 15% tax rate plus 15.3% Social Security tax. This example doesn't take into account any state income taxes that you might need to pay.

Table 2. Worksheet: Take-home pay working outside your home

Income	Kally's numbers	Your numbers
Annual gross salary	$30,000	_____
Employer-paid health insurance	$3,000	_____
Employer-paid retirement contribution	$1,000	_____
Other employer-paid benefits	$0	_____
Total income (wages and benefits)	$34,000	_____
Expenses		
Child care	$4,000	_____
Commuting (gas, parking, bus and train fares, etc.)	$2,000	_____
Work clothing	$1,000	_____
Eating out at work (lunch, snacks, etc.)	$1,000	_____
Miscellaneous work expenses (supplies, dues, etc.)	$200	_____
Taxes (federal, state, Social Security)[a]	$4,500	_____
Other work-related expenses	$100	_____
Total expenses for working outside your home	$12,800	_____
Take-home pay working outside your home	$21,200	_____

a. On this line, enter the taxes from your last tax return; the tax shown for Kally is just an example.

Providing Exempt Child Care

Child care licensing rules vary a lot by state. Some states allow you to care for up to six children before you're required to be licensed or have to follow any state regulations. An *exempt* provider is someone who isn't licensed but is still operating legally because she isn't required to be licensed to operate her program. However, there are some issues that you should consider if you're thinking of operating your business as an exempt provider:

- The IRS treats providers who are exempt from licensing just like licensed providers. This means you will need to keep good business records and report all your income and expenses, just as a licensed provider must. (Exempt providers are entitled to claim all the same business deductions as licensed providers.)

- As an exempt provider, you won't be able to buy business liability insurance to cover your financial responsibility for any children who are injured while in your care. Even if you're only caring for one child, this could still present a significant risk.

• •

A Licensor by Any Other Name

Every state has its own family child care regulations, and the names of the regulations aren't consistent; they may be referred to as *licensing, required* or *voluntary registration,* or *self-certification.* Since *licensing* is the term that is used most widely, this is the term used throughout this book.

• •

Providing Illegal Child Care

If a license is required in your case and you're thinking about operating without it—or if you're planning to care for more children than your licensing rules allow—then your business will be *illegal*, which is something that we strongly oppose. You should understand the serious consequences of this choice; these include the following:

- If you are reported, you may be charged a penalty for violating the law.

- You won't be able to buy business liability insurance to cover your financial responsibility for any children who are injured while in your care.

- If you are sued, the fact that you are operating illegally will be used against you, creating additional liability for you.

- If there is damage to your home or its contents, your homeowners insurance is unlikely to cover the damage.

- If you use your car to transport the children in your care, you probably won't be covered in case of an accident.

- Although you'll still be required to report your business income to the IRS, you won't be entitled to deduct any of the expenses associated with your home, thus greatly reducing the deductions you can legally claim to offset your income.

- Most important, if you are operating illegally, you probably won't be in compliance with the health and safety standards that are designed to help keep the children safe.

Whatever reasons you may have for operating illegally, the costs and risks you run are too great. Don't do it.

Remodeling Your Home for Your New Business

Family child care providers want to have a nice learning environment for the children in their program. To create such a space, you may need to make improvements to your home, such as remodeling a room or adding a deck. (A home improvement is work that increases the value of your home—as opposed to repairs or maintenance, which merely maintains its value.) In addition, your state licensing rules may require you to make specific improvements, such as adding a basement egress window or installing new windows or doors. Before you undertake any home improvements for your new business, you should understand the tax consequences.

Let's say that you're planning to open your new business in a few months, and you decide that the best place for the children to spend their time will be an unfinished room that you want to convert into a playroom. To prepare this room for the children, you'll need to put up new dry wall, paint the walls, install new electrical outlets, and lay down new flooring. You estimate that this will cost you $5,000. You say to yourself, "That seems like an awful lot of money right now—but since I'll be able to deduct it from my taxes, it won't really cost me that much. So I can't lose!"

Not so. The money you spend on a home improvement won't significantly reduce your taxes, since you're required to depreciate this kind of expense over 39 years (and you'll only be able to take the depreciation deduction as long as you remain in business). This means that a $5,000 remodeling project will give you only a $128 annual deduction ($5,000 ÷ 39 = $128). And that's the maximum deduction, which you will only be able to take as long as you use the room exclusively for your business.

If you or your family ever spend time in the room for personal purposes (say, on evenings or weekends), then you won't be able to depreciate that much. Instead, you'll have to multiply the cost of the project by your business-use percent (in this case, your Time-Space percentage) to determine the portion of the expense that you can depreciate.

For example, if your business-use percent is 40%, you'll be able to claim a depreciation deduction of just $51 each year ($5,000 x 40% = $2,000 ÷ 39 years = $51). (For an explanation of the Time-Space percentage and how to calculate your depreciation deduction, see the *Tax Workbook and Organizer* for the appropriate tax year.)

Now that you understand the tax consequences, is the project still worth it to you? The small tax deduction doesn't mean that you shouldn't do the work—it just means that the effect on your taxes shouldn't be a factor in your decision. There may still be excellent reasons to do the remodeling project. You may need to do the work in order to become licensed or to make your home suitable for child care. You may expect that the project will enhance the appeal of your program and help you attract new clients. The project may add to the value of your home, or your own family may appreciate and enjoy the changes you are thinking of making.

Understanding Your Business Tax Deductions

The rule described above for home improvements also applies to all other expenses you incur for your business: *don't spend money just to get a tax deduction.* Why? Because the deductions you're entitled to claim for your business expenses don't reduce your taxes dollar-for-dollar; they simply reduce your profit. Although this lower profit will reduce your taxes to some extent, you will never end up ahead by spending more money.

For example, if you spend $100 on toys for your program, this will reduce your profit by $100, which could reduce your total taxes by as much as $45—but never by the entire $100. The amount you'll save will be based on your total tax rate (federal and state income taxes plus Social Security taxes), which will probably range from 30% to 45%, depending on your family income and the state you live in. So you'll never come out ahead by spending money on business expenses and then deducting those costs on your tax return.

Furthermore, as we've seen, when you incur a large expense—such as a home improvement, an appliance, or a fence—you can't deduct the entire business portion of that expense that year. You'll have to depreciate the expense over several years (the number of years depends on the kind of expense), which will spread the tax benefits over time. As we saw above, home improvements must be depreciated over 39 years, and your tax savings each year will be small. Here are some additional examples of depreciation:

- If you spend $1,500 on a new washer and dryer and use these appliances for both business and personal purposes, you'll have to depreciate their cost over seven years. If your business-use percentage for these items is 40%, you'll be entitled to a business deduction of about $86 a year over the seven years, which will probably save you about $25 in taxes each year.

- If you spend $5,000 to remodel your playroom and you use that room exclusively for your business, you'll be entitled to a business deduction of about $128 a year over 39 years. This will save you only about $40 to $50 in taxes each year, and only as long as you remain in business.

Finally, bear in mind that once you close your business, you won't be able to take any remaining depreciation deductions for that business. So if your family child care business doesn't work out, you'll see very little reduction in your income taxes for any large depreciable expenses that you incurred for your business. (For more information about the tax implications of closing your business, see the *Money Management and Retirement Guide.*)

CHAPTER THREE

Write a Start-Up Plan

Chapter Summary
This chapter explains how to write a start-up plan for a new family child care business. It describes a range of issues that you should address in the planning stages to avoid problems later. This chapter may also be helpful if you are planning an existing business for the first time.

If you're setting up a new family child care business, the first part of your business plan will be your start-up plan, which is intended to help you anticipate and address any issues that could derail your new enterprise. (It may also be helpful to review these issues the first time you plan an existing business.) This chapter will take you step-by-step through preparing a start-up plan. It will show you how to address critical matters:

- any legal or regulatory requirements that could pose an obstacle to your plans
- the start-up costs and start-up funding required for your new business
- the business tax consequences of the decisions you make while starting your business
- the client contract and program policies you will use for your new business

As you read this chapter, you may want to refer to appendix A, which shows both sample and blank start-up plans that you can use as a guide. The blank plan will also be posted on our Web site, www.redleafpress.org—enter "Business Planning Guide" into the search field, and follow the links. You can download the blank plan as a PDF file. (The only software you will need is a PDF reader, which you can download for free if you don't already have it.)

Legal and Regulatory Issues

Before you get very deep into the planning process, contact your child care licensor or local child care resource and referral agency and find out what legal and regulatory requirements will apply to your new business. You want to find out about any potential legal roadblocks *before* you invest a lot of time and money. (To locate your local child care resource and referral agency, visit www.naccrra.net. For more information about legal and regulatory requirements, see the *Legal and Insurance Guide*.)

In this section I will highlight some of the most significant issues that you should check out. However, the rules and requirements vary quite a bit across the country, so some of these issues may not apply to you, and you may need to meet other requirements that aren't listed here. In your start-up plan, note each of the areas that apply to your situation, and describe how you have resolved them. If there are additional requirements that apply to you, add another page listing those rules and explaining how you have resolved them.

Child Care Regulations

In this part of your start-up plan, describe the child care regulations that apply to you and explain how you plan to resolve them.

Before you can open a new family child care business, you'll need to meet all the family child care regulations that apply in your area. Although these regulations vary widely, they may stipulate certain requirements for your home or require you to make safety modifications to your home, such as installing an egress window. You need to make sure that your home qualifies for providing family child care and that you can afford to make any changes required.

Disqualification Factors

In this part of your start-up plan, confirm that you qualify to provide child care in your state.

Many states have a list of "disqualification factors" that they use to screen potential child care providers. These may include a criminal background or a history of mental illness or chemical dependency in yourself or a family member. For example, some providers have had a problem getting licensed because their son or spouse had a run-in with the law years earlier. It's important to identify the "disqualification factors" in your state early in your planning process and make sure you won't have a problem.

Business Name

In this part of your start-up plan, state the business name that you will use and note whether you have registered this name with your state.

You aren't required to adopt a separate name for your business. If you do, most states allow you to use your full name to identify your business ("Melissa Edwards Child Care") without requiring you to fill out any paperwork. However, if you operate under any other business name ("Tiny Tots Child Care"), most states require you to register the name.

To register a business name in most states, you'll need to contact the secretary of state's office, which will check to see if the business name you wish to use is already registered by someone else in the state. If it isn't, you'll be able to register the name for a small fee. For more information, visit the Web site for the office of your secretary of state (or call them).

Legal Structure

In this part of your start-up plan, state whether you will be operating as a sole proprietor. If not, identify the legal structure you will use for your business.

When you open your business, by default its legal structure is a sole proprietorship, which is simply a business operated by a self-employed person. If you wish to remain a sole proprietor, you don't need to take any other steps. As a rule, I recommend that family child care providers operate as sole proprietors.

However, you can adopt another business structure—a partnership, limited liability company (LLC), or corporation. Since these options are far more complicated than operating as a sole proprietor, any change may have significant tax and legal implications for your business. If you're thinking of adopting another business structure, be sure to consult an attorney and a tax preparer first. Also see the detailed discussion of various business structures in the *Legal and Insurance Guide*.

Business Location

In this part of your start-up plan, state the street address where your business will be located, as well as your phone number and e-mail address.

This entry is fairly straightforward. However, if you're thinking of remodeling your home for your business or operating your business outside of your home, consider these alerts:

- If you're considering remodeling your basement or garage in preparation for using those areas in your new business, first check with your licensor to see if your state has any restrictions on using that part of your home in a family child care business.

- If you're thinking of operating your child care business in a building that isn't your home, review the trade-offs discussed in the *Money Management and Retirement Guide* before proceeding further. You may need to consult both an accountant and a tax professional to get a clear picture of the financial impact of this decision.

Housing Barriers

In this part of your start-up plan, confirm that there are no legal barriers to your home business, or explain how you will resolve any barriers that you have identified.

Before opening your business, you'll need to check whether there are any legal barriers to operating your business in your home:

- **Zoning laws**. Do the local zoning laws allow family child care providers to operate in a residential zone? Some areas allow this, while others don't. To find out, check with your licensor or your city or county zoning office.

- **Deed restrictions**. Some private landowners—such as homeowners associations, home developers, and landlords—have either a general deed restriction against operating any business on their property or a specific restriction against operating a family child care business. Read all the deeds and covenants for your property before opening your business (and also before buying a new home in which to continue an existing business).

- **Child care regulations**. Most states have minimum limits for the indoor and outdoor square footage available to children in a family child care business. Your home may also have to pass inspections by the building and fire departments. The regulations may also require certain home improvements, such as adding an egress window or a yard fence. Don't go too far in planning your business without making sure you can afford to make any home improvements needed to comply with the child care regulations.

Start of Business Date

In this part of your start-up plan, state the date that you expect to open your business.

Once you schedule the opening date for your business, let everyone know about it—share it with your friends, family, and other family child care providers. Announce your opening date in the marketing materials that you are using to promote your program.

The biggest unknown in scheduling your opening date may be getting the final approval of your license, especially if it requires approval by the fire or building department; in some areas, these approvals can take months. To help plan your opening date, ask your licensor how long it usually takes to be approved for a child care license in your area.

Some states will allow you to care for one or more children before you have final licensing approval. If you choose to care for children before your license is final, be sure to explain your licensing status to the parents so they aren't misled. However, don't care for any children until you have business liability insurance—and you may not be able to get this insurance until you're fully licensed. I strongly recommend that you not start caring for any children until you are fully covered by a business liability insurance policy.

Food Program

In this part of your start-up plan, confirm that you are participating in the Food Program, and list your Food Program sponsor and representative.

The Food Program reimbursements that you entered in table 1 (in chapter 2) are payments you will receive from the Child and Adult Care Food Program, a federal program designed to help you serve nutritious food to the children. You should join this program as soon as you start caring for children so you can receive these payments. Each month you will submit a claim form showing the number of meals and snacks you have served to the children. Once your form is processed, you will receive a check based on your claim. Depending on the number of meals you have served and other factors, you can expect to get about $2 to $4 per day per child.

Although you must report your Food Program reimbursements as income on your tax return, you will always come out ahead financially by participating in this program because you can deduct the cost of the food you serve to the children in the same way, regardless of whether you're being reimbursed by the Food Program or not.

The Food Program is administered by local nonprofit sponsoring organizations. To find out the sponsors in your area, contact your local child care resource and referral agency.

Start-Up Costs

As a new provider, you'll have to spend some money to get your business off the ground. Start-up costs can vary a lot, depending on your personal circumstances, business goals, and the community you live in. In most cases, the cost of starting a family child care business is pretty low compared to that of other kinds of businesses (unless you're required to make home improvements before opening your business). In general, the more children you plan to care for, the higher your start-up costs will be.

This section lists the expenses that are typically involved in starting a family child care business and explains how to get the money to pay for them. Some of the items listed below may not apply to you, and you may have other start-up expenses that aren't listed; however, this will give you an idea of the kinds of costs you'll need to consider.

Licensing Expenses

In this part of your start-up plan, list the start-up costs that are required to meet the child care licensing requirements for your business.

Your required start-up costs are the expenses you must incur to meet the child care licensing rules and requirements for your state—you can't defer these expenses or open your business without paying them. The list below shows the most common kinds of start-up expenses. Be sure to ask your licensor about the rules in your state, since this list may not cover all the items that are required in your case.

- licensing fees (child care license, local business license)
- smoke detectors or fire extinguishers
- criminal background check
- fire and building inspection fees
- well water test
- medical exam or tuberculosis test
- safety items (outlet covers, child safety locks, a first aid kit, a security gate)
- toys (indoor and outdoor)
- training classes
- vehicle expenses (mileage for trips involved in meeting licensing rules)
- children's activity expenses (books, music, child care curriculum)
- cribs and playground equipment
- home remodeling (providing an egress window, installing a yard fence)

Other Start-Up Costs

In this part of your start-up plan, list the optional costs that will be involved in starting your business, including insurance, equipment, other fees and expenses, and home repairs and improvements.

There will also be some other start-up costs that you may have to pay before starting your business, even if they aren't required for licensing. For example, I strongly recommend that you make sure your homeowners and vehicle insurance policies provide full business coverage and that you buy business property and business liability insurance before you start caring for children (chapter 4 provides a list of all the business insurance coverage that every family child care provider should carry).

Most of these other start-up expenses are at your discretion, and you may be able to defer many of them until you start receiving some income. These optional start-up expenses might include new equipment, home repairs, advertising expenses, office expenses, carbon monoxide detectors, a security system, professional development books and classes, vehicle expenses for business trips, family child care association dues, and business and professional fees (lawyer, accountant).

Reducing Your Start-Up Costs

In this part of your start-up plan, describe how you will keep your start-up costs low.

When starting out, be prudent about buying any items for your business that you don't need right away. One provider advises that you "start small—you don't have to get the best toys and supplies right away to be successful. Get a little at a time, and invest in quality instead of quantity." This is excellent advice. When you begin, just buy a few high-quality items— they'll last longer than cheaper items. You can always pick up more toys and supplies later, once you know what the children really need and you have some income to pay for them.

If there are some items you would really like to have up front, see if you can get them for less than their full retail cost. Here are some strategies for keeping your initial expenses low:

- Check out books, videos, and music CDs from the library.

- Buy used toys and equipment at yard sales or on www.craigslist.org.

- Organize a book and toy exchange with other local family child care providers.

- Ask your local family child care association if they know of any local providers who are going out of business and might have toys or equipment to give away or sell cheaply.

- Instead of buying your own equipment, take the children to a neighborhood playground.

- Shop wisely for food—use coupons, buy in bulk, shop from a list, and avoid prepared foods (they're more expensive).

• •

Don't Spend All Your Money Before You Start!

In planning your start-up spending, bear in mind that you don't want to max out your checkbook on start-up expenses—it isn't a good idea to open your new business with an empty bank account! You'll need to have some cash on hand to cover your operating costs and pay your bills, especially because it may take a while to meet your enrollment goal (as I'll explain in chapter 5).

• •

Sources of Start-Up Funds

In this part of your start-up plan, list the source(s) of the start-up funds for your business.

Although the list of potential start-up costs may look awfully long, the actual cost of opening a family child care business is often relatively low. Many communities don't charge high licensing fees to family child care providers. You may already have most of the toys and equipment you need—or you may be able to obtain them inexpensively. So the cost of getting your business started may be as little as a few hundred dollars.

Nevertheless, once you add up all your start-up expenses, you may realize you don't have enough money to pay for them. Your start-up plan should identify where you'll get the money to pay for these expenses. Here are some potential funding sources:

- your personal savings
- your relatives
- your friends
- a home equity loan from your bank
- a loan from your credit union
- a grant from your local child care resource and referral agency

Notice that I haven't listed credit cards as a source of start-up funds; that isn't an oversight. The high interest rates on credit cards are a trap for anyone who is trying to save money and keep expenses low. In our survey, a sadder-but-wiser provider warned, "*Don't* use credit cards to start your business!" It's okay to occasionally charge small expenses, such as toys, as long as you pay off the entire bill at the end of the month. (For a full discussion of credit card debt and a list of organizations that offer grants and loans to family child care businesses, see the *Money Management and Retirement Guide*.)

Instead of using a credit card, see if you can get a loan; most loans carry far lower interest than credit cards. Check out all the other options first, because a loan should be your last resort. Although other kinds of small businesses often borrow money to get started, a family child care provider should think carefully before taking out a start-up loan. Borrowing a lot of money to start your business may be risky, because you can't be sure of a steady income right away, and many providers operate with a low profit margin.

Business Tax Issues

Some of the decisions that you'll make in planning your new business—such as your start-up spending and the rooms that you will use in your home for your new business—may have significant tax consequences at the end of the year. To avoid problems later, some tax issues should be understood before you set up your business. Reviewing these issues in your start-up plan will ensure that you don't discover their consequences for the first time when you prepare your first-year taxes.

For more information about these issues, see the latest edition of the *Tax Workbook and Organizer*.

Start-Up Expense Deductions

In this part of your start-up plan, list your total start-up expenses in three categories, based on how you can deduct each kind of expense.

You'll probably need to spend some money to open your new business, as explained above. You can deduct these start-up expenses in various ways, depending on the kind of item you buy and when you buy it. Here are the rules for deducting the various kinds of start-up expenses:

- **Items costing less than $100 that you buy for your business before your business begins**. You can deduct up to $5,000 for these items in the first year of your business. You must depreciate any expenses for these items above this $5,000 limit.

- **Items costing more than $100 that you buy for your business before your business begins**. As a rule, you must depreciate these items over several years, as described above. However, you may be able to deduct some of these items in one year, using the Section 179 rule (see the *Tax Workbook and Organizer*).

- **Items you owned before your business began that you didn't originally buy with the intent of using them in your business**. This category is likely to include a wide range of items in your home, such as your sofa, refrigerator, washer, dryer, play equipment, tables, chairs, pots and pans, lawn mower, and any home improvements you have made in the past—in fact, virtually everything in your home. You must depreciate these items as described above. You will need to keep an inventory of these items, as described in the *Record-Keeping Guide*.

For more information about deducting your start-up expenses and depreciating your household items, see the latest edition of the *Tax Workbook and Organizer*.

Home Expenses

In this part of your start-up plan, list any rooms in your home that you don't expect to use on a regular basis in your business.

One of the major financial benefits of opening a family child care business is being able to deduct many of the expenses associated with your home. These deductible expenses include a portion of your utilities, property taxes, mortgage interest, homeowners insurance, home repairs, and home depreciation. Except for property taxes and mortgage interest (which you may be able to claim on **Schedule A**), these expenses represent thousands of dollars that aren't otherwise deductible on your tax return. Claiming these home expenses will significantly reduce your business income and is likely to save you hundreds of dollars in taxes.

To maximize your deductions for home expenses, you will want to use as many rooms in your home as possible for your business on a regular basis. The more space you use regularly for your business, the higher your home deductions will be.

Social Security Taxes

In this part of your start-up plan, confirm that you have included Social Security tax in your first-year budget or income projection.

Many new providers are surprised to discover that they owe Social Security taxes as well as income taxes on their business profits—they may even owe more in Social Security taxes than in income taxes. You may not even have been aware of this tax until now, because an employee only has to pay half of this tax (usually by payroll deduction), while her employer contributes the other half.

However, once you become a self-employed person, you'll have to pay the full amount of this tax yourself. If your **Schedule C** shows a business profit of $400 or more, you'll owe 15.3% of that amount in Social Security taxes. If you have less than $400 in profits, you won't have to pay this tax—but that's not always a good thing, because you must pay Social Security taxes for 10 years in order to qualify for retirement benefits. (For more information, see the *Money Management and Retirement Guide*, which also explains how you will pay your Social Security taxes as a self-employed person.)

The blank budget template in appendix C includes a line for Social Security taxes. To address this part of your start-up plan, simply fill in that line of your budget as directed, and make a note that you have done so in this section of your start-up plan.

Estimated Taxes

In this part of your start-up plan, describe how you plan to pay the estimated taxes for your business.

As a self-employed person, you must pay estimated taxes throughout the year—the IRS won't let you wait until the end of the year to pay the taxes you owe. You're required to pay at least 90% of the tax owed (both federal income tax and Social Security tax) at least every quarter of the year. Check with your state to see if you're also required to pay estimated state taxes during the year. Most family child care providers cover their estimated taxes by using one or both of the following methods:

- Withhold more money from your spouse's paycheck.
- Pay on a quarterly basis by filing **Form 1040ES Estimated Tax for Individuals**.

How much can you expect to owe on your business income? One rule of thumb is that you're likely to owe about 20% of your gross income (your parent payments plus your Food Program reimbursements) in federal taxes. Your actual estimated tax payments will depend on your circumstances. You'll need to consult a tax professional to find out the amount of estimated taxes you'll need to pay each year to avoid a penalty.

If you're paying quarterly estimated taxes, be sure to check the tax deadlines and plan ahead. For example, April 15 is both the last day to pay up for the previous year and the deadline to pay first-quarter estimated taxes for the current year. If you still have some remaining taxes to pay for the previous year, you'll need to save up in advance to meet this double deadline.

Your Contract and Policies

It's important to have a written contract and policies that clearly spell out your rules and expectations to your clients. As one provider advised, "Treat your business as a business, have each family sign a contract, get the tuition in advance, and get paid for holidays and vacations." Since one of the benefits of having your own business is being your own boss, you're free to set your policies and run your business however you like.

Some providers choose to start their business without having parents sign a contract—and almost always they come to regret that decision later. Asking parents to sign a formal contract is essential for communicating your rules, avoiding misunderstandings, and protecting yourself if a dispute arises.

In this part of your start-up plan, you'll write and attach the client contract and policies for your program. Although this may seem like an awfully big task, it really isn't—for two reasons. First, your initial agreements just need to cover the key elements listed below; you can always start with a bare-bones document and expand it later. Don't worry about getting all your rules and terms exactly right—experience will be your best guide, and you'll be able to change, add, or eliminate policies and contract terms whenever you like.

Second, in preparing your contracts and policies you should definitely consult *Contracts and Policies* and use the resources on the CD that accompanies that book. The book discusses all the issues related to contracts and policies in depth, so you'll be able to get quick answers to any questions you have. The files on the CD provide many examples of legal wording that you can copy, paste, and adapt. If you use these resources, you'll be surprised at how quickly you can write up your contract and policies.

Your Contract

In this part of your start-up plan, attach the written contract that you will ask parents to sign, covering (at least) the five areas listed below:

1. The names of the parties
2. Your days and hours of operation or the child's schedule

3. Your fees—the amount, the payment date, and any other fees and expectations. For example,
   - your fees for late payment, late pick-up, registration, bounced checks
   - how you will handle holidays, vacations, and the child's absences
   - the date of your annual fee increase
4. A termination clause
5. The signatures of both parties

To write your contract, consult *Contracts and Policies*, and copy or adapt the legal wording for the contract terms you want to use from the CD that comes with that book.

• •

The Two Most Important Payment Terms

To make sure no private-pay client ever leaves owing you money, I strongly recommend that your contract include these two key terms:

- Parent must pay for child care at least one week in advance.
- Parent must pay for the last two weeks of child care in advance.

If a parent cannot afford to pay you in advance, then set up a payment plan that allows her to pay a little extra each week until you have the advance payment in full.

These two rules should apply to all your private-pay clients. If your state allows you to ask subsidized families for a copayment, ask your subsidy program case worker if you're permitted to require copayments from these clients in advance as well.

• •

Your Policies

In this part of your start-up plan, attach the written program policies you will give to parents, covering (at least) these areas:

- a description of your program activities
- your health and safety rules
- your transportation policy
- your pickup and drop-off rules (car seats, unauthorized pickups, alcohol and drug use)
- your field trip permission form
- your backup care policy
- your behavior guidance policy

To write your policies, consult *Contracts and Policies*, and copy or adapt the legal wording for your policy rules from the CD that comes with that book.

CHAPTER FOUR

Write a Business Plan

Chapter Summary
This chapter explains step-by-step how to prepare the seven elements that are necessary in a business plan for any family child care business.

The previous chapter explained how to write a start-up plan. This chapter explains how to prepare the remaining seven sections of your business plan. As you read the description of each section, it may be helpful to refer to the sample business plan shown in appendix B. That appendix also provides a blank business plan that you can copy and use to get started. This blank business plan will also be posted on our Web site, www.redleafpress.org. (Enter "Business Planning Guide" into the search field, and follow the links.) You can download this PDF file and use it as a template for your own business plan.

Your Hopes and Goals
In this part of your business plan, record your hopes and goals for your business in the coming year.

Your family child care business isn't just about caring for children or earning a living. It's also about you, and you have your own reasons to be in this business—your own hopes, goals, and expectations. Ultimately, this business is your adventure.

In this part of your business plan, briefly jot down some notes that will help you evaluate your progress at the end of the year, based on the factors that are most important to you. If you like, you can list specific hopes and goals for the coming year (profit earned, number of children in care, professional development goal, and so on). Or you can just pose some questions that you'd like to ask yourself at the end of the year:

- Did you have as much fun as you thought you would?
- How did you make a difference in the lives of the children?
- How did doing family child care help your own family grow this year?
- What were the two most important things you learned about yourself this year?

Every year, use these notes or questions to review the previous twelve months, and celebrate your successes by doing something special. Consider whether there's anything that you'd like to do differently in the coming year. Finally, update this section by setting some new goals or revising your review questions.

Your Marketing Plan

In this part of your business plan, describe the steps you're taking to promote your program and keep it fully enrolled.

Identify Your Key Benefits

To promote your program, you need to clearly communicate its benefits to both current and prospective clients. In the marketing sense, a "benefit" is simply a way in which your program is meeting the needs of the children in your care. Think of your benefits as your response to the questions "Why would I want to enroll my child in your program?" and "What does your program offer that others don't?" Your program benefits will be most effective if you can relate them to the mission statement or purpose you have written for your business, as described below (under the program plan).

In this part of your business plan, state the three most important benefits of your program. For example, here are the three benefits listed in our sample business plan:

- I provide an individually designed learning program for each child to help the children learn and grow.

- I offer planned events with two other providers in my neighborhood so the children can play and learn social skills with a variety of other children.

- We are close to a public park that has many child-friendly activities (such as swing sets, a ball field, etc.) for the children to enjoy.

To get some ideas for the specific language you can use to convey the benefits and quality of your program, see the *Marketing Guide,* and check out the accreditation standards on the Web site for the National Association for Family Child Care, www.nafcc.org.

Talk to Your Local Child Care Resource and Referral Agency

Your local child care resource and referral agency has a lot of information that you may be able to use to help promote your program. It's a good idea to contact the agency at least every six months to update the information about your program in its files—your openings, program benefits, and other specifics.

When you call the agency, also ask about the child care needs in your community: What type of care is in greatest demand? How does your program compare to other local programs? Does the agency have any suggestions for how you might attract more clients?

Collect Information about Local Fees and Benefits

To keep your program competitive, you'll need to review your rates and benefits each year and compare them to other child care programs in your area. (I suggest that you raise your rates annually—for more information, see the *Money Management and Retirement Guide*.)

For this review, you'll need to gather information about the fees and benefits of other child care programs in your area. You may also want to keep track of the services that competing programs are offering: Is transportation offered? Are diapers provided? What kinds of field trips are offered? Are evening and weekend services available?

There are two main sources of information about local rates and benefits—other programs and your local child care resource and referral agency. The best approach is to call some child care centers and family child care homes in your area and inquire about their fees and benefits. (Ideally, I'd suggest that you call three child care centers and five family child care homes, as listed in the plan template.)

When you make these calls, don't identify yourself as a child care provider, since federal antitrust law prohibits you from discussing rates with potential competitors. It's fine to ask for publicly available rate information, as long as you don't reveal that you're in the same business. (For more information about what you can and cannot discuss, and with whom, see the *Legal and Insurance Guide*.)

The second approach is to call your local child care resource and referral agency, which usually knows at least the average rates for the family child care homes and child care centers in your area. The agency may also possess averaged data for other kinds of charges, such as paid vacations, registration fees, and late fees. Ask for the range of rates charged by the providers in your area for each age group, and compare your rates to the top 20%.

If the agency doesn't have that information and can only give you average rates by age group, bear in mind that the wide range of child care rates usually makes these averages meaningless. In that case, ask them what the child care centers in your area are charging. Although this will offer only a guideline, you can use it to set a goal of charging roughly comparable rates—especially for infant care, where the competition is the greatest.

Conduct Regular Marketing Activities

Marketing your program is far more than simply buying an ad in your local newspaper. There are many marketing strategies you can try out that won't cost you a lot and will be easy to implement. (The very best marketing for your business is free—it's the word-of-mouth marketing that happens when happy clients tell their friends about your program.) In all your marketing activities, your goal is to communicate the benefits of your program and show potential clients that their children will thrive in your care.

Start by identifying a dozen or more marketing strategies that you'd like to try. Consult the *Marketing Guide* for a comprehensive list of suggestions for marketing your business. Here is a sampling of those ideas to help you get started:

- Give some of your business cards to prospective and current clients, and encourage them to pass the cards on to other parents who may be in need of child care.

- Distribute flyers for your program to people you meet while taking the children on outings (such as to the park) or on field trips.

- Let your current and previous clients know that you'll pay them a finder's fee if they refer a new client who enrolls in your program.

- Create a Web site for your program. (You can do this without any special skills and at no cost using one of the Web site hosting services listed at www.thefreesite.com/Free_Web_Space.)

- Prepare a photo album to show to prospective clients when they come for an interview.

- Record a business message on your voice mail or answering machine.

- Send an e-mail or printed newsletter to your current and prospective clients.

- Hold a celebration—such as a business anniversary party, a summer barbecue, or a holiday party—and invite the families of your current and previous clients.

- Buy advertising in the parents' magazine for your city or state.

Once you have gathered the ideas you'd like to try, create a marketing plan for the next twelve months. In your plan, schedule at least one marketing activity per month. If you fill all your openings, don't stop promoting your program—keep up your marketing efforts in order to build up a waiting list of potential new clients.

Collect Ongoing Feedback

Develop a plan to collect ongoing feedback about your program. Ideas such as the following will help you assess what you're doing right and gather suggestions for areas of your program that you might want to improve:

- Ask parents to complete a written evaluation once a year while in your program and again when they leave your program. Although it will be helpful to have this information in writing, some parents may prefer a spoken interview; in that case, schedule an in-person meeting or phone call, and take detailed written notes.

- Collect feedback about your program from outside sources, such as your local child care resource and referral agency, your Food Program sponsor, your local government subsidy program, and your child care licensor. In these interviews, ask: How is my program different from other programs? What are the unique benefits of my program? What can I do to improve my program?

- If a family has an interview with you but decides not to join your program, make it a practice to send the parents a written survey shortly afterward. In the survey, ask the parents for their impressions of your program and how you might improve it. Enclose a stamped, self-addressed envelope.

Your Insurance Plan

In this part of your business plan, document the insurance policies you're carrying to reduce the risks of operating a business out of your home.

Operating a child care business in your home raises the possibility that a child will be injured in your care, your property may be damaged, or you may be sued. To protect yourself against these risks, you need to *(a)* follow all child care licensing rules; *(b)* follow commonsense rules to keep the children safe; and *(c)* buy adequate insurance. In this section of your business plan, list your insurance policies, giving the name and phone number of your agent, the insurance company, and the policy number.

In this business, being properly insured is not a luxury. If you don't carry adequate insurance, you'll be putting your family, your home, your business, and your financial future at risk. (For more information about buying insurance for your business, see the *Legal and Insurance Guide*.)

All family child care providers should have at least four kinds of insurance coverage:

- **Homeowners**. A homeowners insurance policy will generally cover your home and its contents and also provide some personal liability protection. However, once you start operating a business in your home, some homeowners policies will no longer cover your home or may severely limit your coverage. Check with your homeowners insurance agent to make sure that your home is fully covered. Be sure to get her answer in writing, and file it with your business plan.

- **Business property**. Most homeowners insurance policies have a limit (typically around $2,000) on the amount of business property that is covered. Since most of the household items that you own (such as furniture, appliances, equipment, computers, bedding, pots and pans) will also be used in your business, you'll need to make sure that you have a business property insurance policy that will fully cover those items. For more information, contact your homeowners or business liability insurance agent.

- **Vehicle**. Your vehicle insurance policy may not cover the use of your car for business purposes. Therefore, it's essential to check with your vehicle insurance agent and get a written guarantee that you're still covered when using your car to transport the children and during other business trips without the children, such as shopping for supplies, visiting yard sales, and driving to the bank. (I'll explain vehicle insurance further below.)

- **Business liability**. Every family child care provider should have business liability insurance to protect herself from lawsuits and other incidents that can arise in her business.

Finally, there is one more kind of insurance policy that you may want to consider:

- **Disability income**. A disability income insurance policy replaces some of your income if you are disabled and unable to earn a living. Child care is physically a very demanding job, and the risk of becoming disabled is real. Nevertheless, most providers don't carry this kind of insurance, and it isn't as essential as the policies listed above.

Make Sure Your Vehicle Is Fully Covered

If you're using your vehicle for your business, you're probably already aware of the problem of obtaining adequate and affordable vehicle insurance.

- If you use your car or van on a regular basis for your business, your insurance company may cancel your coverage, refuse to cover a claim that you file, or require you to buy commercial insurance, which costs a lot more than regular insurance. (You may even be required to get a commercial driver's license.)

- If you use your vehicle only occasionally for your business, you may not need any additional insurance, but you do need to confirm that you are covered with your insurance company.

The most important point is to make sure you will be covered in case of an accident. Talk to your vehicle insurance agent, and explain exactly how you use your car or van in your business. Describe all the ways that you transport the children (or may transport them)—such as driving to the park, school, or library; field trips; and emergency trips. Describe all the ways you use your vehicle for business when the children aren't with you—for making bank deposits, going to garage sales, going shopping, or driving to training workshops.

If you're told that you're fully covered for all of these trips, *get this assurance in writing*. If you aren't fully covered, you may want to consider not transporting the children in your car anymore. Or you can try shopping around for another policy that will cover you. Our site provides an insurance directory to help you find insurance coverage for your vehicle. Go to www.redleafpress.org, enter "Business Planning Guide" into the search field, and follow the links.

Your Program Plan

In this part of your business plan, describe the purpose or goal, choices, and curriculum of your child care program.

Purpose or Mission Statement

It can be very useful to give your clients a brief statement of your purpose for doing child care or the overall goal (mission) of your business. This statement can be helpful in conveying your benefits and distinguishing your program from other programs. It's also a way to educate parents about the issues that are most important to you. Here are some examples:

- your views on child development
- the importance of religion or values in your work
- your goals for the children in your program

Your purpose or mission statement can be brief, summed up in a single sentence: "I run a child-centered program that focuses on meeting the individual needs of each child." Or your statement can be longer, if you want to explain your views in detail. It's up to you.

Program Choices

In this section, document the decisions you've made in the following areas:

- **The number and ages of children you'd like to care for**. Continue to reassess this decision as you gain experience, the children in your care grow older, the demand for child care shifts in your area, or your preferences evolve.

- **Any rooms that will be off-limits to your program**. Some providers like to set aside some areas for their own children and spouse to use. For example, will your child's bedroom or your own bedroom be accessible to the children in your care? Although each room or area that you put off-limits will reduce your business deductions, as described in the previous chapter, you may feel that your family's privacy is a reasonable trade-off.

- **Any rooms that will be used 100% for your business**. Using one or more rooms in your home exclusively for business offers a major tax benefit, as described in the previous chapter. However, to claim this deduction, you'll need to set aside the space (such as a playroom, bedroom, or storage area) for business and never use it for personal purposes.

- **Whether you will hire any employees**. Hiring an employee to help care for the children is a complex decision that will have far-reaching consequences. Before you pay anyone to help you care for the children, refer to the *Money Management and Retirement Guide* to determine how many more children you'll need to care for to make it worthwhile.

Child Care Curriculum

Family child care providers are instrumental in promoting the growth and development of the children in their care—this is what distinguishes them from babysitters. Some providers like to design their own curriculum for their program. Others prefer to use a commercially prepared curriculum to help design learning activities for the children.

Whether you use an informal or a formal curriculum, you should regularly let the parents know what you're teaching their children. If you don't feel comfortable using the word *curriculum* because you don't have a formal written lesson plan, you can say that you offer an "individual, play-based program that uses teachable moments to help children learn."

Redleaf Press offers several curriculum books you can use to develop activities for your program. For more information, visit www.redleafpress.org and enter "curriculum" into the search field, or call us at 800-423-8309.

Your Professional Development Plan

In this part of your business plan, describe your plan for building on your child care skills to achieve your professional development goals.

It's your responsibility to provide the best possible care for the children enrolled in your program. This means following all the applicable child care regulations—in particular, the requirements for professional development. Research shows a direct correlation between high-quality child care and the provider's professional training. Furthermore, a 2002 family child care report showed that a provider's education level had a significant effect on her business. Each year of additional education increased her fees an average of $3 a week.*

No training is required before you begin offering child care. Fifteen states require some training during the first year of operation. Seventeen states require at least 12 hours of annual training after that. (For more information about state child care licensing requirements, visit www.naccrra.org/randd/licensing_training_qr/family_cc_provider_training.php.)

Since these are the minimal training requirements, we recommend that you make it a priority to set a professional development goal each year that exceeds your state's requirements. For information about training opportunities in your area, contact your local child care resource and referral agency or your local family child care association.

Professional Education and Credentials

If you plan to work in family child care for more than a few years, we recommend that you think seriously about obtaining a professional credential, certificate, or degree in early childhood education. Many state subsidy programs pay a higher rate to providers who have achieved certain professional credentials, and you can use your credential or education as a basis for charging higher fees to your private-pay clients:

- **National Association for Family Child Care Accreditation**. This credential certifies that your program meets quality standards in the areas of relationships with parents and children, child care environment, developmental learning activities, safety and health, and professional and business practices. For more information about this credential, visit www.nafcc.org, or call 800-359-3817.

- **National Child Development Associate (CDA) credential**. This credential certifies that you are able to meet the specific needs of children, including their physical, emotional, and intellectual growth, in a child development framework. For more information about this credential, visit www.cdacouncil.org, or call 800-424-4310.

- **Degree or post-secondary courses in early childhood education**. Your local community college, technical school, or university may offer classes or degrees in early childhood education. For more information, contact the schools in your area.

Although it's not directly related to your child care skills, it's also a good idea to include some business training in your professional development plan.

---

* S. W. Helburn, J. R. Morris, and K. Modigliani, "Family Child Care Finances and Their Effect on Quality Incentives," *Early Childhood Research Quarterly* 17, no. 4 (2002): 512–38.

If you choose to pursue one of these educational objectives, include it in your professional development plan as a long-term goal, and then track your progress each year. The importance of getting the proper training was emphasized in this comment in our survey:

Most of the family child care providers I know who have failed didn't have the proper training. My nine years have been very successful. I have my CDA and NAFCC accreditation, and have done very well.

Professional Organizations

Another sign of professionalism is joining one of the professional organizations for family child care providers, such as the National Association for Family Child Care (NAFCC) or a state or local family child care association.

Most professional associations offer resources to help their members improve their child care skills by offering opportunities for training, mentoring, and networking. Many of these organizations offer other benefits, including discounts, newsletters, and advocacy.

For more information about NAFCC, visit their Web site, www.nafcc.org, or call 800-359-3817. To find out about other family child care associations in your area, contact your licensor or your local child care resource and referral agency.

Your Record-Keeping Plan

In this part of your business plan, describe your plan for keeping your business records and tracking your program data.

In this part of your business plan, you'll describe the record-keeping system that you'll use to track your income and expenses. There are three major reasons why it's essential to have a solid record-keeping plan for your business:

- You're in business to make money. Good records will tell you how well you're doing and whether you're making progress toward your financial goals. Without good records, you may not know how you're doing, which will make it difficult to make wise financial decisions. Good record-keeping is also necessary for financial planning, such as preparing a budget (see chapter 5).

- At the end of the year, parents may request a receipt for their child care payments that year in order to claim the child care tax credit on their federal tax return. To provide this information, you'll need to keep track of all the payments you've received from parents.

- Since parents will be paying you for child care, the IRS considers you to be operating a child care business, even if you are unlicensed, bartering for child care, or operating illegally. This means that you'll need to file a federal income tax return to report your business income (including the value of any services you have bartered). Good records are the only way to determine exactly how much tax you should be paying—no more and no less. Good records decrease the likelihood that you will be audited, and if you are audited, they will be your basis for defending your return.

What Information Do You Need to Track?

A good record-keeping system tracks the following information throughout the year:

- daily attendance for each child
- payments from parents
- Food Program reimbursements and monthly claim forms
- business expenses (receipts, cancelled checks, credit and debit card statements)
- the number of hours you work in your home
- your business insurance policies
- your child care contracts (the original documents, signed by you and the parents)
- your federal and state tax returns
- your monthly bank statements (for both business and personal accounts)
- your employee records (payroll, employer taxes, personnel, and training records)
- your corporate bylaws and other corporate records, if your business is incorporated

Although the above list covers the most important records that most child care providers need to keep, it may not include everything you'll need to track. For example, to support your tax deductions, you may need to track your use of some items used for both business and personal purposes. For more information, see the *Record-Keeping Guide*.

Choosing a Record-Keeping System

There are many resources available to help you choose a record-keeping system and maintain your records. One good place to start is the latest edition of the *Record-Keeping Guide*, which explains everything you need to know about record-keeping for a family child care business. However, that book is only the first step in an integrated series of comprehensive record-keeping and tax preparation resources available from Redleaf Press. You can choose the record-keeping tools that work best for you and keep your records either electronically or on paper. At the end of the year, this integrated system will make it easier to file your tax returns.

To track your records, you might choose either the *Redleaf Calendar-Keeper* or *CK Kids* software. Both of these resources allow you to track all your records; the main difference between them is that the *Redleaf Calendar-Keeper* is a printed system in which you enter information by hand, while *CK Kids* allows you to keep your records electronically:

- The *Redleaf Calendar-Keeper* includes monthly income and expense charts that allow you to organize your business income and expenses as they occur. To complement this record-keeping resource, you can also use the *Family Child Care Mileage-Keeper* to track your mileage, the *Family Child Care Inventory-Keeper* to track the depreciable household items used in your business (such as furniture, appliances, and equipment), and the *Family Child Care Business Receipt Book* to record payments from parents.

- *CK Kids* software allows you to track your income and expenses and print out monthly, quarterly, and annual reports showing your net profit or loss. The annual reports make it much easier to fill out your tax forms.

You can choose either method. One provider in our survey wrote, "I highly recommend the *CK Kids* program—it's so easy to get your totals at the end of the year!" To learn more about this software, visit www.minutemenu.com/web/mmkids.html.

• •

Preparing Your Taxes

At the end of the year, you have two options for doing your taxes. You can do them yourself, following the instructions in the *Tax Workbook and Organizer* for that tax year. Or you can hire a tax preparer and use the *Family Child Care Tax Companion* to make sure that she doesn't make any mistakes or leave out any deductions that you're entitled to claim. (The *Tax Companion* is designed to help you communicate with your tax preparer and educate her about the unique tax rules that apply to family child care businesses.)

• •

Do You Need a Business Checking Account?

Although a separate business checking account may be helpful for tracking your expenses and keeping your financial records, this isn't required by the IRS. A second checking account takes more time to manage, and it still won't keep your business and personal finances completely separate. As long as you're working out of your home, there will always be some overlap between your business and personal expenses. If you do want to keep these two areas as separate as possible, here is what you need to do:

- Deposit all your business income (parent fees, government subsidies, Food Program reimbursements, etc.) into your business checking account.

- Write checks on your business account for all your business-only expenses (such as supplies and toys).

- Write checks or transfer money into your personal account to pay your own "salary" and to pay for the business portion of your recurring home expenses.

Some banks charge more for a business checking account than for a personal one. To avoid this extra cost, just open a second personal account for your business and tell the bank it's your "home" account (if it asks). If you have a business name ("Wonder Years Day Care"), don't put it on your checks, and ask parents to write their checks to your name, not to your business name. (Otherwise your bank may start charging you extra fees.)

Your Financial Plan (Budget)

For this part of your business plan, attach an annual budget to plan the financial side of your business. (For help in preparing a family child care budget, see chapter 5.)

There are many reasons to prepare a financial plan (annual budget) for your business:

- If you're just starting out, a first-year budget shows you if you can expect to make a profit in the first twelve months.

- If you've been in business for a while, preparing an annual budget each year helps you to plan for the future and keep your expenses under control.

- In operating your business, regular budgeting helps you keep up the small steps that are needed to stay on track toward your long-term financial objectives, such as your retirement savings.

- You can also use your budget to explain your business to the parents, calculate your hourly wage, find your break-even point, and create a monthly cash flow projection—all of which are described in chapter 6.

Yes, a budget is truly a wonderful thing. However, who likes to prepare a budget? Apparently, very few of us. Only 23% of the providers in our money management survey said they had prepared a budget for the previous year. Yet when we asked them to give some advice to other providers for getting a better handle on their money, they repeatedly recommended budgeting as the most important step:

Budget!

Make a budget, and stick to it.

Write out a budget. You'll be surprised by how much money you really have when you pay attention to it.

Make a budget. Project your income for the next year based on your lowest monthly income over the last twelve months.

Set up a separate checking account for your business. This has helped me keep track of my expenses and stay on a budget.

Treat your business as a business. Each month, put away some cash, and educate yourself about making and following a budget.

Invest the time to set up a budget spreadsheet to track your business and personal finances. The more you're aware of your money, the more control you'll have over where it's going.

Despite these voices of experience, most providers still aren't using a budget. Why? Probably for many reasons. Some people don't want to plan ahead, especially if they're embarrassed about how they're spending their money. Other people feel too stressed, ashamed, or powerless to change their financial situation. Some people have never tried to budget, don't know how to start, and are afraid it will be unpleasant and difficult. You can probably think of many more reasons.

However, it's never too late to learn some new habits and skills. If you try making a budget, you may discover that it isn't as difficult as you expected—and that the time you spend doing your first budget will be well worthwhile. In fact, you should see an obvious payoff. A budget can improve your ability to control your finances; it can:

- show you whether you are on track to meet your current financial expectations
- help you keep your expenses under control by "pre-thinking" your spending decisions
- help you resist the temptation to make an impulse purchase
- show you how well you've done so far
- show you whether you can afford to buy something new for your business
- provide a guideline for spending your money over the year

Bear in mind that your budget doesn't need to be locked in stone—if your financial circumstances change, you may need to make some adjustments. For example, you may need to revisit your budget if a parent leaves owing you money or if it takes a while to fill an opening in your program. However, it's also true that you'll get the most out of your budget if you're able to follow it closely enough to reach your planned financial goals for the year.

Ideally, you'll prepare a new budget each year. When it comes time to redo your budget, take the opportunity to review your business plan and evaluate your progress toward your long-term goals. If you'd like to make any changes to your business, such as increasing your income or the size of your program, you can experiment with the next year's budget (and the financial tools described in chapter 6) to find the best way to implement that change. In the words of one provider in our survey,

> *If you don't know how to do the accounting for your business, learn. Any professional in any business should know where the money comes from and where it goes. Learn to do a budget and a cash flow statement. Figure out what kind of family or type of care will give you the most income for the services you provide.*

Should You Combine Your Personal and Business Budgets?

Once you experience the benefits of budgeting your business, you may want to budget your personal finances as well. Your personal budget includes your personal expenses and any income you receive from other sources, such as your spouse or ex-spouse, Social Security, investments, or rental property. You can either do a separate personal budget or merge your business and personal finances into one form.

If you have one budget for both your personal and business finances, you can see your entire financial situation at a glance. However, there are some drawbacks to this approach. For example, this may make it more difficult to focus on carefully managing your business expenses. To decide whether or not to merge your budgets, ask yourself which benefit is most important to you—being able to see your entire financial picture at once or keeping your business finances separate so you can track them more carefully?

Use a Budgeting Tool

Appendix C provides a blank template for a family child care budget, and chapter 5 explains how to prepare a budget for your business. However, as you get further into budgeting, you'll probably find it very helpful to use one of the many online tools and software programs designed to help people budget and manage their money.

Although the best-known money management programs are Quicken and Microsoft Money, you may not need all the features offered in those programs, and many other programs focus specifically on budgeting. Some of these tools are free, and the others generally offer a free trial period. A budgeting tool can remind you when your bills are due and help you balance your checkbook, track your bank accounts and credit cards, watch your expenses by category, and set monthly limits by spending category.

If you haven't tried to use a budget before, I suggest you do some experimenting and find the tool that works best for you. Here are some that you may want to check out (most of these programs are free):

- Buddi: buddi.digitalcave.ca
- ClearCheckbook: www.clearcheckbook.com
- Crown Mvelopes: www.crown.mvelopes.com
- YNAB Pro: www.youneedabudget.com

CHAPTER FIVE

Prepare a Budget

Chapter Summary
This chapter provides a sample family child care budget and explains how to prepare a budget and estimate the business income and expenses for a new family child care business.

If you're just starting out in family child care, it's important to get into the habit of budgeting your business from the start. To help you do that, this chapter explains how to prepare a budget for your new business. I'll provide a sample budget that you can copy; I'll also explain how to estimate your own numbers, which you can enter into a copy of the blank budget form shown in appendix C. You can also download a copy of the blank budget form from our Web site, www.redleafpress.org. (Enter "Business Planning Guide" into the search field, and follow the links.)

I'm directing this chapter at beginning providers, because it's more difficult to do a budget for a new business. If you're preparing a budget for an ongoing business, just ignore any sections that don't apply to you. The process is the same, except that it is easier to come up with your budget numbers, since you have some history on which to base them.

The Sample Budget

Table 3 shows a sample of a first-year budget for a new family child care business. As you can see in this example, a budget basically involves estimating your income and expenses, subtracting your total expenses from your total income to get your net profit before taxes, and then subtracting your taxes to get your net profit after taxes.

Most of the lines on this budget are self-explanatory, and you can follow this outline, substituting your own numbers for those shown here. However, be sure to read the notes at the end of the table, since they point out some assumptions I have made that may not apply to you and explain how to calculate your own numbers on those lines. In your budget, you may also need to add some lines for items I didn't include (such as other kinds of fees that you charge), or delete any lines that don't apply to you (such as the business loan expenses).

Table 3. Sample budget

Income			
Income from parents			
Infants: $175/week x 50 weeks x 1	$8,750		
Toddlers: $145/week x 50 weeks x 2	$14,500		
Preschoolers: $135/week x 50 weeks x 3	$20,250		
Total		$43,500	
Program fees			
Registration fees: $25 per family x 6		$150	
Food Program income[a]			
$1.82 per child per day x 5 days/week x 50 weeks x 6 children		$2,730	
Gross income			$46,380
Income reductions[b]			
Partial enrollment reduction (20%)	$9,276		
State subsidy program clients (5%)	$2,319		
Missed payments (2%)	$928		
Provider sick days (2%)	$928		
Total		$13,451	
Net income ($46,380 − $13,451)			$32,929
Expenses			
Business supplies			
Children's supplies	$960		
Food	$5,670		
Toys	$500		
Household supplies	$840		
Other supplies (such as for special field trips)	$100		
Total		$8,070	
Other business expenses			
Professional development	$350		
Advertising	$152		
Vehicle[c]	$604		
Depreciation of household items (furniture, appliances, etc.)	$420		
Business liability insurance	$750		
Office expenses	$480		
Repairs of toys, furniture, and equipment	$100		
Total		$2,856	
Home expenses[d]			
Property tax	$1,200		
Mortgage interest	$1,200		
Utilities	$600		
Home repairs	$350		
Homeowners insurance	$600		
Business property insurance	$100		
Home depreciation or rent	$1,400		
Total		$5,450	

Table 3 *(continued)*

Business loan (for start-up expenses)			
Repayment of principal	$550		
Loan interest	$160		
Total		$710	
Other expenses			
Employees	$0		
Total		$0	
Total expenses ($8,070 + $2,856 + $5,450 + $710 + $0)			$17,086
Net profit before taxes and retirement contribution[e] (net income – total expenses: $32,929 – $17,086)			$15,843
Retirement contribution		$2,000	
Net profit after retirement contribution[f]			$13,843
Taxes			
Social Security taxes[g] ($15,843 x 15.3%)		$2,424	
Federal income taxes[h] ($13,843 x 15%)		$2,076	
State income taxes[i]		$0	
Total		$4,500	
Net profit after taxes (net profit before retirement – total taxes: $15,843 – $4,500)			$11,343
Cash on hand at the end of the year (net profit after taxes – retirement contribution: $11,343 – $2,000)			$9,343

a. Here I'm using the 2007–2008 Tier II Food Program rates—$1.82 per child per day (for serving breakfast, snack, and lunch). For your budget, project your reimbursements for the upcoming year based on the current rate that applies to your program.

b. Since these reductions are percentages of gross income, note that they reduce both parent fees and Food Program income.

c. Here I'm using the 2008 IRS mileage reimbursement rate (86 miles/month x $0.585); for your budget, use the current mileage rate.

d. To get the totals to enter in this section, multiply your actual home expenses by your Time-Space percentage. The provider in our example has a Time-Space percentage of 40%; if you aren't sure what your Time-Space percentage should be, you can use the example's percentage as a ballpark estimate for your first year.

e. Use this number to calculate your Social Security taxes.

f. Use this number to calculate your income taxes.

g. If net profit before taxes is greater than $400, enter 15.3% of that total on this line; otherwise, enter 0.

h. Here I'm using 15% of net profit after the retirement contribution; see a tax professional for the amount you should budget for federal income tax.

i. This example doesn't take into account any state taxes; see a tax professional for the amount you should budget for state income tax.

Although the sample budget includes a line for employee expenses, most new providers don't have employees. If you wish to estimate the costs involved in hiring an employee and add them to your budget, see the *Money Management and Retirement Guide*.

Most of this chapter will explain how to determine your own numbers to enter into the budget form. Before we move on, it's important to understand how this budget projects your income.

How This Budget Projects Your Income

In the income section of this budget form, you'll start by entering your best-case scenario —all the income you receive if your program is fully enrolled and you receive your full fees for the entire year. After adding up that best-case scenario to get your gross income, you'll enter some reductions (as a percentage of your gross income) to take into account some possible reasons that you may not receive the full amount. You'll subtract those reductions from your gross income to get your net income, which is a more realistic estimate of the income you can expect that year.

For example, in the sample budget, I made the following reductions to the provider's gross income to get the net income for her first year in business:

- a 20% reduction for a delay in achieving full enrollment during her first year in business

- a 5% reduction for the possibility that she may be asked to provide care to families who qualify for a state subsidy (The state subsidy payments won't cover her entire fee, and she isn't allowed to refuse to provide care to a subsidized family. However, if her state allows her to charge a copayment that covers the difference between her regular rate and the subsidy rate, then she can omit this reduction. If she expects to care for many subsidized families, she may wish to increase this reduction.)

- a 2% reduction for payment problems, such as a bounced check, the bank overdraft charges for the bounced check, or a parent who leaves without paying her in full

- a 2% reduction for days when she is sick and unable to provide child care

If you aren't sure how much to allow for reductions to your income, I suggest that you use the above reductions for your own first-year budget. If you're certain that one of these reductions won't apply to you, then you can omit it. However, for most people "I just won't get sick" (for example) isn't a realistic plan.

The purpose of a budget is to prepare a realistic picture of the most likely scenario for the coming year. Therefore, it's better to budget conservatively than to plan based on hopes or "stretch goals" that you may not be able to attain.

You may need to include most of the income reductions in your ongoing budgets as well. Once you achieve full enrollment, you may be tempted to drop the 25% partial enrollment reduction in your next budget. However, I suggest that you still include some kind of partial enrollment reduction (perhaps 10%), in case a client leaves unexpectedly and it takes more time than you anticipate to fill that space in your program.

Budget Conservatively

Whenever you prepare a budget, it's important to make conservative assumptions. This means taking into account anything that may reduce your income or raise your expenses.

For example, unless you already have firm commitments from parents to fill your program, you don't want to project full enrollment for your first year in business. As one provider advised, "Don't expect to have the full number of children you're legally allowed to care for at first."

Depending on your neighborhood, the local economy, and other factors beyond your control, it may take anywhere from a few months to more than a year to reach your ideal enrollment level. There's no magical way to estimate how long it will take to fill all the spaces in your program.

To budget conservatively, you should also assume that you won't receive all the income you charge to parents—you may receive some bad checks or run into a client who leaves without paying. Another provider suggested, "Budget just 80% of your income; otherwise one bad check could really mess you up." Budgeting for these kinds of problems doesn't mean that you don't expect the best of your clients—this is just a way to make sure you're prepared for any unexpected shortfalls in your income.

Estimating Your Income

You probably have some questions about how to estimate your income for a realistic budget. New providers often wonder how they can budget their first-year income if they aren't even sure how much they'll be able to charge yet.

Deciding what to charge for your services is one of the most important decisions that you face when you're starting out—and it requires careful thought and a bit of detective work. To set your rates properly, you need to research the prevailing rates in your area. Although it's illegal to discuss child care rates with other local providers, you can find out what others are charging by following the approach outlined in chapter 4.

Once you have gathered information about the rates in your area, consult the in-depth discussions of setting rates and terms of payment in the *Marketing Guide* and *Contracts and Policies*.

Although you don't want to set your fees either too high or too low, bear in mind that more providers go out of business because their rates are too low than because their rates are too high. This section discusses some issues that you should consider in estimating your income—charging by age group; offering discounts, sliding fee scales, and scholarships; and providing care for subsidized families.

Table 4. Worksheet: Family child care rate scale

Age group	Number of children		Weekly fee		Total by age group
Infants	___	x	_____	=	_____
Toddlers	___	x	_____	=	_____
Preschoolers	___	x	_____	=	_____
Schoolagers	___	x	_____	=	_____
Total					_____

Set Your Rates by Age Group

In setting your rates, bear in mind that the fees you can charge will vary based on the age of the child. As a rule, you will be able to charge the most for infants and progressively less for older children through the toddler, preschool, and elementary school years. In order to estimate your first-year income accurately, you'll need to break down your fees by the age groups that you plan to care for. Then use a rate scale worksheet, such as the one shown in table 4, to add up your weekly income at full enrollment.

Multiple-Child Discounts

Some providers offer a second-child or multiple-child discount to attract new clients or to avoid losing an existing client when a new child arrives in the family. It's true that child care is a significant financial burden for many families and another child can create a major burden on the family budget. For this reason, you may be asked (or just feel pressured) to offer a discount for a second child. Before you agree to do so, I urge you to pause and think about what the discount would mean for your business:

- First, you have no economies of scale (ways to save money) when caring for more than one child from a family. Your expenses per child (for food, supplies, etc.) will be just as high for the second child as for the first child.

- Second, your workload won't be any lower for the second child. It will take just as much effort to care for the second child as for the first child. (Some providers may disagree with this and claim that caring for a second child from the same family is less work—but I wouldn't suggest that you assume this to be the case.)

- Finally, add up all the income you'll lose by offering a permanent discount. For example, if you give a $10 weekly discount for the second child, you will lose $520 every year that the child remains in your care. If you hope to care for the child for many more years, your loss could amount to several thousand dollars.

If you'd like to help out a family with a new baby, you'd be better off offering a temporary discount for the second child—for three to six months, say. This will reduce the long-term

Table 5. Sample sliding fee scale

Full rate	Weekly Rate
Family income above $60,000	$150
Sliding scale	
Family income:	
$40,000–$59,999: $20/week discount	$130
$20,000–$39,999: $30/week discount	$120
$10,000–$19,999: $40/week discount	$110
Below $10,000: $50/week discount	$100

financial impact on your business while still easing the family's short-term financial burden during their period of adjustment.

Keeping your rates low or offering discounts isn't the best way to keep good clients from leaving your care. The best approach is to continuously enhance and promote the quality of your program and to communicate the true value of the services you are providing to parents, regardless of what you are charging. (For more information, see the *Money Management and Retirement Guide*.)

Sliding Fee Scales

In setting your rates, you may have considered offering a sliding fee scale or scholarships to make your program more affordable for low-income, private-pay families. If you want to offer a sliding fee scale, you need to make sure that you're treating everyone who is in the same financial situation equally.

Your rate schedule should be public, and it should be based on a clearly stated standard, not just on the empathy (or lack of it) you may feel for a particular parent when she tells you that she can't afford your fees.

If you're adding the sliding scale after your business has started, you may assume that the change will be welcomed by your existing clients who qualify for the new discounts and ignored by the other parents—but that won't necessarily be the case. The way you structure the new fee scale may make a big difference in how well it will be accepted and in whether all the parents feel that they have been treated fairly.

The best approach is to start by making your regular rate the highest rate in your new scale; then offer progressive discounts from that rate for lower family incomes. Table 5 gives an example of how to do this.

In introducing the sample scale shown in table 5 to parents, you can explain your new policy by saying, "My regular rate is $150 a week, but I offer progressive $10 per week discounts for families whose income is below certain limits." This approach makes more sense—and will probably be received more favorably—than establishing a base rate for low-income parents and charging progressively more for higher-income families.

When you make this change, show your new fee scale to the parents of each child in your care, and ask them to identify the payment category that their family qualifies for. That's all you need to do—don't ask your clients for evidence of their income level to prove that they are eligible for a discount.

Scholarships

I find that few providers actually offer a formal sliding fee schedule. More often, they simply offer a temporary scholarship to a specific family that is experiencing a financial emergency, such as a parent losing a job or having a medical crisis.

In such situations, you might choose to reduce your rates, or not charge at all, for a limited time. These informal, temporary scholarships are easier to manage than a sliding scale, and they are likely to cost you less in the long run. To be fair to all your clients, try to base your scholarships on a consistent standard, even if it's simply an unwritten policy that you will try to support families who are having an economic crisis. That way, you'll still be treating all families who are in similar circumstances equally, even though this method is more private than a sliding fee scale.

• •

You Can Charge Different Rates Based on Financial Need

If you are wondering if it's legal to offer different rates to certain families based on financial need, the answer is yes. It's perfectly legal to treat parents differently, as long as the difference isn't based on one of the categories protected by antidiscrimination laws, such as race, color, gender, religion, age, national origin, or physical disability. Some areas of the country also outlaw discrimination based on other categories, such as sexual orientation. For an in-depth discussion of antidiscrimination regulations, see the *Legal and Insurance Guide*.

• •

State Subsidy Payments

To budget accurately, you'll need to plan for the possibility that you'll be caring for some children from low-income families who qualify for a state or county child care subsidy program. (In most states, it's illegal to refuse to provide child care to a subsidized family, although you can ask your licensor about the rules in your state.)

When you care for a child whose family qualifies for a subsidy, the state or county pays you directly for the child's care. However, to receive payment for your services, you'll need to follow all the program's rules, and the parents will need to file the proper paperwork on time. So be sure to find out how the local program works by asking your subsidy program case worker or your child care resource and referral agency the following questions:

- What are the deadlines for the parents to submit their paperwork?
- When you can expect to receive payment?
- What fee will you receive?
- Are you permitted (or required) to charge the parents a copayment?

Since the subsidy payments will probably be lower than what you'll be charging your private-pay clients, your budget should include a reduction to income for the lower fees you are likely to receive for these clients.

Your subsidy program may allow—or even require—you to charge subsidized families an additional copayment that may offset the gap between the subsidy payment and your regular rates. If the copayment you are allowed to charge makes up for the gap between your regular rate and the subsidy rate, then you don't need to include this income reduction in your budget.

If you're charging a copayment, be sure to clearly communicate to parents when their copayments are due and the consequences if they miss a payment deadline. In addition, your contract should stipulate that the family is liable for your entire child care fee if the subsidy program fails to pay you for any reason. (For the specific wording of this term in your contract, see *Contracts and Policies*).

• •

Should You Charge Private-Pay Clients the Subsidy Rate?

Some family child care providers set the regular rate for their private-pay clients at the same level as the subsidy rate paid by their county or state. I don't recommend that you do this.

Government subsidy rates are usually lower than the average fees that providers charge private-pay clients—and in some areas, the subsidized rates are far, far lower than average. Subsidy rates generally don't include annual cost-of-living increases—in fact, some states have frozen their rates for many years.

Finally, if your state allows (or requires) you to charge a copayment in addition to the subsidy, this shows that the state is aware that its reimbursement doesn't cover the full cost of child care and expects you to charge an additional fee.

• •

Estimating Your Expenses

If you're preparing your first-year budget, your business probably isn't open yet. You may not have any previous experience in the child care business, and this may be the first time that you've ever tried to prepare a budget. This lack of experience can make it quite intimidating to even think about trying to forecast your future expenses. It's true that projecting your expenses is probably the most difficult part of preparing a first-year budget. But don't worry—I'm going to give you a shortcut to make this process much easier:

1. Start by estimating your expected first-year income, since that will be easier than estimating your expenses. As described above, estimate your gross income based on full enrollment, and then reduce that total to arrive at a more realistic net income total (as shown in the sample budget).

2. Multiply your total first-year net income by 55% to get your estimated total first-year expenses. Enter that amount on the budget line for total expenses.

3. Fill out the remaining budget lines: deduct your total expenses from your net income to get your net profit before taxes and retirement contribution, and continue from there.

For example, in our sample budget the total net income is $32,929. To use this shortcut instead of estimating individual expenses, we multiply $32,929 by 55%: $32,929 x .55 = $18,111. We enter $18,111 on the line for total expenses, and our net profit before taxes and retirement contribution then becomes $14,818 ($32,929 − $18,111).

Depending on your personal situation, you may want to adjust your ratio of expenses to income up or down based on factors such as the number of children you plan to care for, your cost of housing, the cost of living in your area, and your personal spending habits. You may also want to try estimating your actual expenses line-by-line on the budget, and then use the 55% ratio as a benchmark to see if your total seems reasonable.

• •

Should You Include Your Start-Up Costs?

You don't need to include all your start-up costs in your first-year budget. Although most of your start-up items will be one-time expenses, others (such as your business insurance) will be recurring expenses each year. You can leave your one-time start-up expenses out of your first-year budget, but I suggest that you include any recurring start-up expenses in your first-year budget, since you will need to include these items in your subsequent budgets.

• •

After the First Year

It will be easier to calculate your expenses for your second-year budget, because by then you'll have some actual history of what it takes to run your business. If you wish, you can recalculate each expense line in your budget—start with your actual cost the year before and add any increases you expect for the coming year.

However, if you aren't planning any major changes to your program, you can simply take your actual (not budgeted) total expenses from the previous year and add a cost-of-living increase for inflation. (If you don't know the current inflation rate, you can use a guesstimate of 4%.)

Should Your Budget Show a Loss?

Don't be alarmed if your first-year budget shows a loss. It's not unusual to lose money in your first year or two in the child care business. The three most common reasons for a first-year loss are high start-up expenses, a delay in reaching full enrollment, and the learning curve involved in starting a new business. (It takes time to learn how to manage your expenses, collect your fees on time, and run a smooth operation.)

However, you don't want to continue to show a loss year after year. For one thing, operating at a loss for years will attract the attention of the IRS and make it much more likely that you'll be audited and have your deductions challenged. (The IRS will wonder if you're really trying to run a business and make a profit or if you just have an expensive hobby.)

Another reason you want to make a profit is that you'll need to report a profit of at least $400 for 10 years in order to qualify for the minimum Social Security retirement benefits. (For more information, see the *Money Management and Retirement Guide.*)

The most important reason you don't want to show a loss every year is that you want to make some money for all your hard work. So here are some ways that you can plan ahead to minimize your chances of a first-year loss:

- Ask your licensor and other local providers how long it is likely to take you to reach full enrollment (this can vary a lot by community). Set the income reductions in your budget to take this delay into account.

- Keep your start-up expenses low, and make sure you have some cash reserves on hand when you open your business, in case your operating expenses are higher than expected.

- Keep your expenses under strict control until you reach your break-even point.

For an explanation of the break-even point and how to calculate it, see chapter 6; for an extensive list of ways to reduce your expenses and increase your income, see the *Money Management and Retirement Guide.*

CHAPTER SIX

Manage Your Business Finances

Chapter Summary
This chapter describes how to use your business budget to help communicate
with your clients, calculate your hourly wage and break-even point, and prepare
a cash flow projection for the coming year.

Once you have prepared an annual budget, whether for a start-up or an ongoing business,
you can use it to manage your business more effectively in many ways. This chapter outlines
four of these options:

- Use your budget to explain your business finances to your clients so they will have a
  better understanding of your rates and fees.

- Calculate your hourly wage to get a true idea of the financial return you're receiving for
  your efforts.

- Find the break-even point for your business so you'll know how many children you need
  to care for to make a profit.

- Prepare a cash flow projection to make sure you will have enough money to pay your
  bills each month and enough time to plan ahead for any shortfalls.

Help Parents Understand Your Business

Many providers find that family child care is not a lucrative business. Our sample budget in
the previous chapter provided a realistic financial profile of a provider who expected to realize over $30,000 in income and yet made less than $12,000 after taxes.

Your clients are unlikely to understand the financial realities of your business; they may
mentally multiply whatever they're paying you by the number of children they see around
your home and assume that you must be making out like a bandit. It can be very helpful to
use your budget to improve their understanding of your business finances and show them
why you charge what you do.

One way to do this is to create a pie chart in Excel to help explain where your money goes through percentages of your expense categories. (If you prefer, you can also draw a rough chart by hand.) Here's how to create an Excel pie chart using the numbers from our sample budget as an example:

1. Open a new spreadsheet, and enter the expenses and net profit from your budget as shown below. The first column is optional—it's just there to help you see what you're entering. Don't include any totals—the numbers you enter should add up to your total income after reductions. In the example below, the numbers shown add up to $32,929, which is the net income after reductions in our sample budget.

Expenses	Business supplies	8070
	Other business expenses	2856
	Business loan	710
	Home expenses	5450
	Retirement contribution	2000
Taxes	Income taxes	2076
	Social Security taxes	2424
Profit	Profit after taxes	9343

2. Select the two right-hand columns:

Expenses	Business supplies	8070
	Other business expenses	2856
	Business loan	710
	Home expenses	5450
	Retirement contribution	2000
Taxes	Income taxes	2076
	Social Security taxes	2424
Profit	Profit after taxes	9343

3. If you don't see the Chart toolbar, select View > Toolbars > Chart to make it appear.

4. On the Chart toolbar, click on the down arrow next to the Chart Type icon, and select Pie Chart from the drop-down menu (the names of the charts appear if you hover your mouse over the icons). That should create a default pie chart that looks something like this (although your chart will be in color):

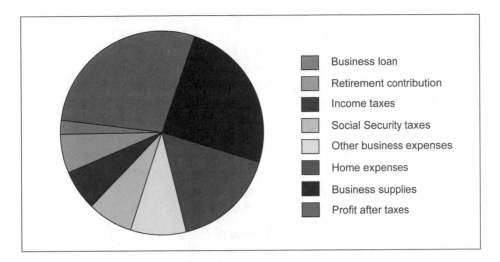

5. You now have a basic pie chart that you can show parents. If you'd like to customize your chart a bit further, you can right-click on various parts of the chart to see menus that will allow you to add a title, change the colors, rotate the chart, add labels, pull out a slice you want to highlight, and so on. (Use the Help menu to find out more.) For example, in a few minutes you can customize the above chart to look like this:

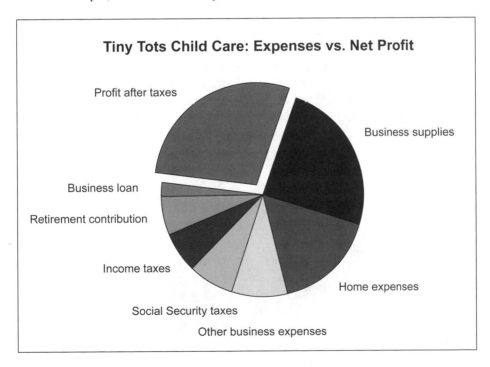

You don't have to indicate how much you have spent on the various expense categories or reveal your business profit. The idea is simply to show the parents that you are keeping a relatively small percentage of the money you are earning (28% in this example).

If you don't want to give parents this much information about your finances, another way to educate them is to share your hourly wage with them (see below). The basic idea is that parents who understand the financial realities of your business are a lot less likely to grumble about paying your fees.

Calculate Your Hourly Wage

Once you have completed a budget and calculated your estimated net profit, it takes only a few more simple steps to figure out how much you're earning per hour doing family child care. There are many reasons to take the time to do this:

- Your hourly wage is the best measure of the relationship between the effort you're putting into your business and the amount you're being paid.

- Knowing your hourly wage helps you set financial goals and understand your financial situation more clearly.

- Calculating your hourly wage is likely to motivate you to find ways to raise your income.

Calculating your hourly wage only requires two numbers—your net profit before taxes and the number of hours you worked that year. You can calculate your hourly wage at the end of a year based on your actual numbers, or you can calculate it for a budgeted year using your projections for that year. The calculation process is the same in either case—just be sure to use your net profit and total hours for the same year. The example below is based on the numbers in the sample first-year budget shown in chapter 5.

Although figuring out your hourly wage takes just one step, you'll first need to add up your total working hours for the year. To get an accurate hourly wage, you'll have to include all the hours you spent (or you expect to spend) on business that year. Here's how to proceed:

1. Add up all the hours you'll be caring for children during the year. For example, let's say your first-year child care schedule will be Monday through Friday from 7 AM to 6 PM, and you plan to take two weeks off for unpaid holidays and vacations that year. In that case, your total child care hours for the year will total 11 hours per day x 5 days a week x 50 weeks: 11 x 5 x 50 = 2,750 child care hours.

2. Add up all the additional time you'll be spending on business activities when the children aren't in your care. If you're just starting out, this may be difficult to estimate. However, on average, family child care providers spend an additional 14 hours per week on other business tasks, such as cleaning, preparing activities, and keeping records. (Don't include any tasks that you do while the children are in your care—if you clean the playroom or

file your receipts while the children are napping, that time has already been included in your child care hours.) For this example, let's assume your additional business time will amount to 14 hours per week, like that of the average provider. In that case, your additional business time for the year will total 14 hours x 50 weeks: 14 x 50 = 700.

3. Add together your total child care hours and your additional business time for the year: 2,750 child care hours + 700 additional business hours = 3,450 total work hours for the upcoming year.

4. To calculate your projected hourly wage, divide the net profit before taxes shown on your budget by your total work hours that year (from step 3). For example, the net profit before taxes in our sample first-year budget is $15,843. Since this provider expects to work 3,450 hours in her first year, her hourly wage that year will be $4.59 ($15,843 ÷ 3,450 hours = $4.59).

At the end of the year, you can figure out your actual net profit and hours worked for that year, and then recalculate your hourly wage and see how close it was to your projection. It's always a good idea to compare your budget to your actual results—this final step will help you budget more accurately the next year.

How to Increase Your Hourly Wage

It can be very helpful to track your hourly wage over time, because this is the number that most clearly shows the relationship between the effort you are putting into your business and the financial rewards you're receiving for your time. Whenever your hourly wage goes up, you're getting a raise! For this reason, your hourly wage is a good benchmark to use for setting your financial goals. Here's how you might use your annual budget to set a goal to make more money per hour.

Going back to our example, let's say that you have now been in business for a full year. It turns out that you did great the first year—you reached your full enrollment goal by the end of the year and actually made about $6 an hour! Now you're preparing your second-year budget, and you'd like to see what it will take to raise your hourly rate from $6 an hour to $8 per hour. Here's how to do that:

1. Check if the total working hours you calculated for last year (step 3 above) will change in the coming year. If that total won't be changing, then you can use it again. For this example, we'll assume that your total hours haven't changed, so we'll use 3,450 hours again. However, if you're planning to change your child care schedule for the new year, or if your estimate of additional working hours wasn't accurate, then you'll need to recalculate your total hours for the new year by repeating steps 1–3 above.

2. Multiply your hourly wage goal by your total working hours for the year: $8 x 3,450 hours = $27,600. This is what your net profit will need to be to make $8 per hour for the number of hours you're currently working.

3. Add to your net profit goal the total expenses you've budgeted for the new year. For this example, we'll simply add a 4% inflation adjustment to the total budgeted expenses for the first year—$17,086 x 1.04 = $17,769. The sum of your total expenses and your net profit is the net income after reductions that you'd need to reach your hourly wage goal: $27,600 + $17,769 = $45,369.

4. Multiply the number of children in care by the number of weeks worked in the new year. Using the assumptions in our sample budget, we get 6 children x 50 weeks = 300.

5. Divide the net income goal ($45,369) by that last number: $45,369 ÷ 300 = $151.23.

The last number calculated in step 5 tells us that you will need to make an average of about $151 per week per child (after income reductions) to make $45,369 in net income and meet your hourly wage goal.

Once you know how much net income you want to make, you don't necessarily have to raise your rates to reach that goal—there are a wide range of options that you can explore to increase your income. For example, you may be able to reach your hourly wage goal by raising your rates a modest amount while implementing a few of the following options:

• Increase the number of children in your program.
• Adjust the ages of the children in your program (for example, by adding another infant).
• Adjust the rates you're charging for certain age groups (or start charging by age group).
• Care for more part-time children, charging a higher daily rate for part-time care.
• Look for ways to reduce your expenses.
• Add program fees, or increase your existing fees (late fees, trip fees).
• Start charging for your vacations.
• Increase your marketing efforts to fill any empty spaces and build a waiting list.
• Get more training to justify charging more for your services.

These are just a few ideas to get you started; for many more suggestions for increasing your income, see the *Money Management and Retirement Guide*.

Find Your Break-Even Point

Another valuable way to use your annual budget is to determine the break-even point for your business. This is the point at which your income begins to cover your expenses so you start making a profit. (The break-even point for a start-up business may not occur for a year or two.) You can also track your break-even point each month to help you stay disciplined and keep your expenses as low as possible, especially if it's taking you a while to reach the overall break-even point for your business.

Although most family child care providers know the maximum number of children that they *want* to care for, it's also important to know how many children you *need* to care for to cover your expenses. By projecting your break-even point, you can find out how many children you need to care for to make a profit. Here's how to calculate your break-even point:

1. Calculate your annual income per child. Divide your gross income (before reductions) by the number of children in your care. Using the numbers in our sample budget, this would be $46,380 ÷ 6 = $7,730.

2. Take your total home expenses ($5,450 in our example) and subtract from it your expenses for home depreciation ($1,400) and business property insurance ($100): $5,450 − $1,400 − $100 = $3,950.

3. Take your total expenses ($17,086) and subtract from them the number you calculated in step 2: $17,086 − $3,950 = $13,136.

4. Figure out how many children it will take to reach the number you calculated in step 3: $7,730 + $7,730 = $15,460. Since $15,460 is more than $13,136, in this scenario, it will only take two children to reach break-even and start making a profit.

Note: You may also want to use the online break-even calculator available on our Web site, www.redleafpress.org. (Enter "Business Planning Guide" into the search field, and follow the links.)

There are two times when it's especially important to calculate your break-even point— before starting your business and whenever you have significant change in your business income or expenses. Keeping track of your break-even point will help you avoid running your business at a loss for an extended period. If you see that you won't be able to break even the way you're operating your business, you can look for ways to increase your income or reduce your expenses right away, instead of waiting until the end of the year.

Prepare a Cash Flow Projection

Once you're comfortable with preparing a budget and feel ready to add another financial planning tool, the next logical step is to project your monthly cash flow by breaking down your budgeted income and expenses by month.

The purpose of this cash flow projection is to show you exactly how much money you expect to have—and to need—each month. You can use this tool to identify when your expenses are due and to make sure you'll have enough cash on hand to pay them. A cash flow projection is also very helpful when you want to apply for a loan, because it documents the monthly profits you expect to make and shows that you are managing your business finances in a professional way.

Whether you're a new or experienced provider, projecting your cash flow can be very helpful in gaining better control of your business finances. Some providers do a cash flow projection every year, along with their budget. Others only do it for the first year or two they are in business to make sure that they get off to a good start.

Appendix C shows a sample cash flow projection. To create your own cash flow projection, you can start by downloading the blank Excel spreadsheet posted on our Web site, www.redleafpress.org. (Enter "Business Planning Guide" into the search field, and follow the links.)

After downloading the spreadsheet, you can adapt it and enter your own numbers. If you prefer, you can use Excel or another spreadsheet program to design your own cash flow projection form from scratch. You can even do a cash flow projection by hand (as long as you check all your totals carefully).

Although it has an impressive-sounding name, a cash flow projection really isn't all that complicated to do, especially if you let the spreadsheet software add up all the totals for you. There are really just three steps involved:

1. Spread your budgeted income by month.
2. Spread your budgeted expenses by month.
3. Deduct your expenses from your income, and review your cash flow each month.

1. Spread Your Income

Start your cash flow projection by breaking down the income totals in your annual budget by month. Enter each monthly amount in the month in which you expect to receive it, not the month in which you expect to earn it. (You want to know when you'll actually have the cash on hand.) For example, in the sample cash flow projection in appendix C, I assumed that the provider is paid on Monday, so I counted the number of Mondays in each month to determine her total income for the month.

In spreading your income for the next year, consider your plans for that year:

- If you plan to take an unpaid vacation during the year, remember to reduce your income from parents and the Food Program that month. (Although many providers don't charge for their vacation time, you certainly can do so—for more on this topic, see the *Money Management and Retirement Guide*.)

- If you expect to have lower enrollment during the summer months, reduce your income from parents and the Food Program for those months.

- If you know that a family will be leaving your program in the next year, reduce your income from parents and the Food Program for a month or two after the family's last day, in case you aren't able to fill the space right away.

- If you plan to raise your rates during the year, include this increase in your projected income.

In the sample cash flow projection, I assumed that the provider would receive her Food Program reimbursements one month after filing her claims. Since this is a first-year scenario, we don't show any Food Program income for her first month in business (January). We show the Food Program claim that she files in January as income in February, and the claim that she files in February as income in March—and so on, going forward. I also assumed that the provider was receiving the lower Tier II reimbursement rate. (To project this income, I used the 2007–2008 rates for the first half of the budgeted year and assumed that the rate would rise by 3% for the second half of the year.)

2. Spread Your Expenses

Next, break down your budgeted expenses by month, and enter each expense in the month in which you expect to pay for it.

- Some expenses, such as food, toys, and supplies, will be fairly consistent from month to month. For these expenses, you can start by dividing your annual total by 12 and entering the result in each month. Then see if you need to make any adjustments for months in which your expenses will be higher or lower than usual.

- Other expenses, such as business liability insurance, home repairs, and quarterly estimated tax payments, will be infrequent or irregular; enter those expenses in the month in which they are due.

3. Review Your Monthly Cash Flow

For each month, deduct your estimated expenses from your estimated income to see how much money you will have left at the end of the month. If you notice a month in which your expenses will exceed your income, you can plan how to handle that gap well in advance, perhaps by saving a bit more in the preceding months. Using your monthly cash flow projection helps you to avoid surprises at the end of the month, decide whether (and when) you can afford to purchase new items, and reduce the temptation to spend money when you can't afford to.

If you notice that your income consistently exceeds your expenses, you can plan how to use that surplus—for example, by making contributions to your emergency and retirement funds. Be careful not to conclude that you have extra money to spend just because your income exceeds your expenses for a few months. Look ahead to upcoming months, and make sure you'll have enough money saved to pay your quarterly estimated taxes and large bills that only fall due once or twice a year, such as your insurance and property taxes.

• •

Remember to Pay Yourself!

The new provider who created our sample cash flow projection had planned to pay herself each month by withdrawing some money as a personal "draw" on her profits. However, in doing her first-year cash flow projection, she realized that she would have to wait for a few months before she could start taking a draw. She projected that she would be able to take her first draw in March and gradually increase it as her cash on hand accumulated.

• •

Keep Your Cash Flow Projection Updated

By projecting your budgeted cash flow by month, you're actually converting your annual budget into a monthly budget. Doing a new 12-month cash flow projection at the same time as your annual budget each year will help you refine your annual budget, making it much more realistic and accurate. When you spread your income and expenses by month, you're likely to notice many small adjustments that you forgot to account for in your annual totals, and these small adjustments can add up.

It can be very helpful to keep updating your projection as your income and expenses change during the year. Keeping an ongoing, updated cash flow projection will help you manage your money and make it much easier to plan your next budget. If you do this, you may even want to prepare your cash flow projection for the coming year first, then add up those monthly numbers to get the totals for your annual budget.

In the example above, we assumed that you created your budget first and based your cash flow projection on the budgeted totals. Although this is probably the easiest method at first, as you gain experience, you may find it easier to build your budget up from your actual cash flow by month. It's fine to do it either way.

As the months go by, be sure to compare your actual income and expenses to the projections made in your annual budget and monthly cash flow projection. If you see that you're consistently failing to meet your financial goals, look for ways to reduce your expenses, increase your income, or promote your program more aggressively. (For suggestions, see the *Money Management and Retirement Guide* and the *Marketing Guide*.) Once the year is over, take the time to look back at the budgets and projections you made over the year. You'll probably find that you have learned a lot about your business and significantly improved your ability to plan and manage your business finances.

APPENDIX A

Start-Up Plans

Blank Start-Up Plan

••

Instructions: Fill in the blanks and check the boxes that apply to you, adding any further details or explanation as needed. To answer "no" to a question, simply leave that box unchecked.

••

Legal & Regulatory Issues
Child Care Regulations

_____

_____

Disqualification Factors
❑ I am qualified to provide child care in my state.

Business Name
❑ I have a business name: _____
❑ Business name is registered with the state? Registration number _____

Legal Structure
I will operate my business as a

❑ sole proprietorship (self-employed business)
❑ partnership
❑ limited liability company (LLC)
❑ S corporation
❑ C corporation

Business Location
Address _____
Phone number _____
E-mail _____

Housing Barriers
❑ Business is in compliance with local zoning laws.
❑ Business is not prohibited by deed or landlord restrictions.
❑ Child care licensing rules allow me to operate in my home.
❑ Child care licensing rules require home improvements to open my business.

Start of Business Date: _____

Food Program
❑ I am participating in the Food Program.
Name/phone number of sponsor _____
Name of representative _____

Start-Up Costs

Licensing Expenses (specify or explain as needed)

The following start-up costs are required for my business:

- ❑ $_____ Licensing fees _____
- ❑ $_____ Smoke detectors/fire extinguishers _____
- ❑ $_____ Criminal background check _____
- ❑ $_____ Fire/building inspection fees _____
- ❑ $_____ Well water test _____
- ❑ $_____ Medical exam/tuberculosis test _____
- ❑ $_____ Safety items _____
- ❑ $_____ Indoor toys _____
- ❑ $_____ Outdoor toys _____
- ❑ $_____ Training classes _____
- ❑ $_____ Vehicle expenses _____
- ❑ $_____ Children's activity expenses _____
- ❑ $_____ Cribs/playground equipment _____
- ❑ $_____ Home remodeling _____
- ❑ $_____ Other _____

Total licensing expenses: $_____

Insurance

- ❑ $_____ Business property policy
- ❑ $_____ Commercial vehicle insurance
- ❑ $_____ Business liability insurance
- ❑ $_____ Disability income insurance

Equipment (specify as needed)

- ❑ $_____ Car seats _____
- ❑ $_____ Cribs/cubbies _____
- ❑ $_____ Children's furniture _____
- ❑ $_____ Other _____

Fees and Expenses (specify as needed)

- ❑ $_____ Children's activity expenses _____
- ❑ $_____ Family child care association dues _____
- ❑ $_____ Advertising _____
- ❑ $_____ Office expenses _____
- ❑ $_____ Security system _____
- ❑ $_____ Business fees _____
- ❑ $_____ Professional fees _____
- ❑ $_____ Vehicle expenses _____

Home Repairs and Improvements (list)

❑ $____ _____
❑ $____ _____
❑ $____ _____

Other (list)

❑ $____ _____
❑ $____ _____
❑ $____ _____

Total other start-up costs: $_____

Total start-up costs: $_____

Plan for Keeping Start-Up Costs Low

_____
_____

Sources of Start-Up Funds

❑ $____ Personal savings
❑ $____ Relatives
❑ $____ Friends
❑ $____ Home equity loan
❑ $____ Credit union loan
❑ $____ Grant from my child care resource and referral agency
❑ $____ Other *(specify)* _____

Total funds available for start-up costs: $_____

Business Tax Issues

Start-Up Expense Deductions

Total of items costing less than $100 and bought before my business began _____

Total of items costing more than $100 and bought before my business began _____

Total of items owned before my business began and used in my business _____

❑ I am keeping an inventory of the household items used in my business (see the *Record-Keeping Guide*).

Home Expenses

❑ All the rooms in my home will be used regularly in my business.
❑ The following rooms will not be used regularly in my business _____

Social Security Taxes

❑ Social Security taxes of 15.3% are included in my first-year budget or profit estimate.

Estimated Taxes

- ❑ I will pay my estimated taxes on a quarterly basis by filing **Form 1040ES** on April 15, June 15, September 15, and January 15 each year.
- ❑ My spouse will withhold enough money from his paycheck to cover my estimated taxes.
- ❑ Other *(describe how you will pay your estimated taxes)* _____
_____

Contract

My written contract is attached. My contract contains:

Contract Terms (specify as needed)

- ❑ The names of both parties _____
- ❑ My days/hours of operation _____
- ❑ Termination clause _____
- ❑ Signatures of both parties _____

Fees (specify as needed)

- ❑ Parents must pay at least one week in advance _____
- ❑ Parents must pay the last two weeks in advance _____
- ❑ Payment date listed _____
- ❑ Late payment fee _____
- ❑ Late pickup _____
- ❑ Registration fee _____
- ❑ Bounced check fee _____
- ❑ Holding fee _____
- ❑ Paid holidays _____
- ❑ Paid vacation _____
- ❑ Paid for child absences _____

Policies

My written policies are attached.

- ❑ Program activities _____
- ❑ Health and safety rules _____
- ❑ Responsibility as a mandated reporter of child neglect _____
- ❑ Privacy policy _____
- ❑ Transportation policy _____
- ❑ Pickup and drop-off rules _____
- ❑ Field trip policy _____
- ❑ Backup care rules _____
- ❑ Behavior guidance policy _____
- ❑ Date of annual rate increase _____

Sample Start-Up Plan

Legal & Regulatory Issues

Child Care Regulations

I must put an egress window in my basement if I want to use it as a playroom. Because I have a play area upstairs, I won't make this improvement until there are six children in my program.

Disqualification Factors

☑ I am qualified to provide child care in my state.

Business Name

☑ I have a business name: Little Lambs Child Care

☑ Business name is registered with the state? Registration number: 887341

Legal Structure

I will operate my business as a

☑ sole proprietorship (self-employed business)

❑ partnership

❑ limited liability company (LLC)

❑ S corporation

❑ C corporation

Business Location

Address: 1770 Hampshire Ave, St. Paul, Minnesota 55117.

Phone number: 555-233-7777

E-mail: littlelambs@aol.com

Housing Barriers

☑ Business is in compliance with local zoning laws.

☑ Business is not prohibited by deed or landlord restrictions.

☑ Child care licensing rules allow me to operate in my home.

❑ Child care licensing rules require home improvements to open my business.

Start of Business Date

January 1, 2008

Food Program

☑ I am participating in the Food Program.

Name/phone number of sponsor: Community Coordinated Child Care, 555-233-2233

Name of representative: Rosalee Wilkins

Start-Up Costs

Licensing Expenses

The following start-up costs are required for my business:

☑ $25   Licensing fees

☑ $120   Smoke detectors/fire extinguishers

☑ $30   Criminal background check

☑ $65   Fire/building inspection fees

❑   —   Well water test

❑   —   Medical exam/tuberculosis test (covered by my medical insurance)

☑ $45   Safety items: outlet covers, child safety locks, first aid kit, security gate, etc.

☑ $250   Indoor toys: games, dress-up clothes, dolls, etc.

☑ $575   Outdoor toys: balls, climber, used tricycles, etc.

☑ $50   Training classes

☑ $75   Vehicle expenses: 145 miles to buy start-up items x $0.52 per mile

☑ $125   Children's activity expenses: arts and crafts, sand, water toys, etc.

☑ $230   Cribs/playground equipment: crib, cot, crib mattress, etc.

❑   —   Home remodeling

☑ $45   Other: repair stair railing

Total licensing expenses: $1,635

Insurance

☑ $110   Business property policy

❑   —   Commercial vehicle insurance

☑ $575   Business liability insurance

❑   —   Disability income insurance

Equipment

☑ $75   Car seats

❑   —   Cribs/cubbies (included above)

☑ $235   Children's furniture

☑ $270   Other (rocking chair)

Fees and Expenses

☑ $130   Children's activity expenses: books, music, curriculum, etc.

☑ $100   Advertising: finder's fee for referring clients

☑ $35   Family child care association dues

☑ $70   Office expenses: *CK Kids* software

❑   —   Security system

❑   —   Business fees

☑ $250   Professional fees: tax preparer

☑ $78   Vehicle expenses: 150 miles x $0.52

Home Repairs and Improvements

❑ — N/A

Other

☑ $45 Rent carpet cleaner
☑ $75 Corner wall guards
☑ $35 Radon and lead testing kit
☑ $60 Paint play room

Total other start-up costs: $2,143

Total start-up costs: $3,778

Plan for Keeping Start-Up Costs Low

• I have bought most of my toys and equipment used at yard sales.
• I will check out books and videos from the library.
• For the time being, I will take the children to the playground instead of buying playground equipment.

Sources of Start-Up Funds

☑ $1,278 Personal savings
❑ — Relatives
❑ — Friends
❑ — Home equity loan
❑ — Credit union loan
☑ $1,000 Grant from my child care resource and referral agency
☑ $1,500 Other: Loan from First Children's Finance (7% interest over 4 years)

Total funds available for start-up costs: $3,778

Business Tax Issues

Start-Up Expense Deductions
Items costing less than $100 and bought before my business began: $285
Items costing more than $100 and bought before my business began: $850
Items owned before my business began and used in my business: $11,500
☑ I am keeping an inventory of the household items used in my business (see the *Record-Keeping Guide*).

Home Expenses
☑ All the rooms in my home will be used regularly in my business.
❑ The following rooms will not be used regularly in my business _____

Social Security Taxes
☑ Social Security taxes of 15.3% are included in my first-year budget or profit estimate.

Estimated Taxes

☑ I will pay my estimated taxes on a quarterly basis by filing **Form 1040ES** on April 15, June 15, September 15, and January 15 each year.

☐ My spouse will withhold enough money from his paycheck to cover my estimated taxes.

☐ Other *(describe how you will pay your estimated taxes)* _____

Contract

My written contract is attached. My contract contains:

Contract Terms

☑ The names of both parties

☑ My days/hours of operation

☑ Termination clause: parents must give a two-week notice.

☑ Signatures of both parties

Fees

☑ Parents must pay at least one week in advance

☑ Parents must pay the last two weeks in advance

☑ Payment date listed: payment is due the Friday before the next week begins

☑ Late payment fee

☑ Late pick up

☑ Registration fee

☑ Bounced check fee

☑ Holding fee

☑ Paid holidays: New Years Day, July 4th, Labor Day, Thanksgiving Day, Christmas Day

☑ Paid vacation: one week in July

☑ Paid for child absences

Policies

My written policies are attached.

☑ Program activities

☑ Health and safety rules

☑ Responsibility as a mandated reporter of child neglect

☑ Privacy policy

☑ Transportation policy

☑ Pickup and drop-off rules: car seats, unauthorized pickups, alcohol and drug use

☑ Field trip policy

☑ Backup care rules

☑ Behavior guidance policy

☑ Date of annual rate increase: rates will be raised on the enrollment anniversary

APPENDIX B

Business Plans

Blank Business Plan

....

Instructions: Fill in the blanks and check the boxes that apply to you, adding any further details or explanation as needed. To answer "no" to a question, simply leave that box unchecked.

Family child care business plan for _____

Hopes and Goals

Hopes

_____

_____

_____

Goals

_____

_____

_____

Marketing Plan

Program Benefits

1. _____
2. _____
3. _____

Child Care Resource and Referral (CCR&R) Updates

❏ I have updated my CCR&R in the last six months about my openings.
My last CCR&R update was on _____

Market Rate Information Survey

	Infants	Toddlers	Preschoolers	Schoolagers
Home 1	_____	_____	_____	_____
Home 2	_____	_____	_____	_____
Home 3	_____	_____	_____	_____
Home 4	_____	_____	_____	_____
Home 5	_____	_____	_____	_____
Center 1	_____	_____	_____	_____
Center 2	_____	_____	_____	_____
Center 3	_____	_____	_____	_____

Marketing Activities

January	_____
February	_____
March	_____
April	_____
May	_____
June	_____
July	_____
August	_____
September	_____
October	_____
November	_____
December	_____

Feedback

❏ I will ask my clients to complete a written evaluation this year in _____.

I will collect feedback about my program this year from my

❏ CCR&R   *When* _____

❏ Food Program sponsor   *When* _____

❏ Government subsidy program   *When* _____

❏ Child care licensor   *When* _____

Insurance Plan

Homeowners Insurance Policy

Insurance company _____   Policy # _____

Insurance agent _____   Phone # _____

❏ I have written proof that my home is fully covered while I am operating a business in my home.

❏ I have written proof that my homeowners policy fully covers the contents of my home used in my business (my business property).

Business Property Insurance Policy

❏ My homeowners policy doesn't fully cover the contents of my home used in my business. My business property insurance coverage is provided by

Insurance company _____   Policy # _____

Insurance agent _____   Phone # _____

Vehicle Insurance Policy

Insurance company _____ Policy # _____

Insurance agent _____ Phone # _____

❏ I have written proof that I am fully covered for all business uses of my vehicle, both when transporting children and on other business trips.

Business Liability Insurance Policy

❏ I don't have this insurance; I'm not covered for business liability risks.

Insurance company _____ Policy # _____

Insurance agent _____ Phone # _____

Disability Income Insurance Policy

❏ I don't have this insurance; I'm not covered for loss of income due to disability.

Insurance company _____ Policy # _____

Insurance agent _____ Phone # _____

Program Plan

Purpose or Mission Statement

_____

_____

Program Choices

Goal for number of children in each age group:

	Full-time	Part-time
Infants	_____	_____
Toddlers	_____	_____
Preschoolers	_____	_____
Schoolagers	_____	_____

❏ Any rooms off-limits to children *(list)* _____

❏ Any rooms used 100% for business *(list)* _____

❏ Plan to hire any employees

Child Care Curriculum

❏ Self-designed curriculum
If not, source of curriculum _____

Professional Development Plan

My Background, Training, and Skills

_____

_____

Professional Development Goal for the Coming Year

_____

_____

Professional Organizations

❑ Member of local family child care association
   Name of association _____
❑ Member of National Association for Family Child Care
❑ Member of any other professional organizations *(list)*

_____

Record-Keeping Plan

I will track the following information *(describe where you record or file the information and how often you update your records):*

❑ each child's daily attendance _____
❑ payments from parents _____
❑ Food Program reimbursements and claim forms _____

   _____

❑ business expenses (receipts, cancelled checks, credit or debit card statements) _____

   _____

❑ hours worked in my home _____
❑ business insurance policies _____
❑ child care contracts _____
❑ federal and state tax returns and quarterly estimated tax payments_____

   _____

❑ monthly bank statements (business and personal accounts) _____

   _____

❑ I have a separate business checking account.
   Name of bank _____ Account # _____
❑ I have employees. I track my payroll records (tax records, personnel records, training records) by _____
❑ My business is incorporated. I keep records of my corporate bylaws and other corporate records by _____
❑ Other records *(list)* _____

_____

Financial Plan

(Attach a copy of your budget; you can use the blank budget in appendix C as a guide.)

Sample Business Plan

Family child care business plan for Little Lambs Child Care

Hopes and Goals

Hopes

I hope to have as much fun caring for the children in my program as I do caring for my own children.

Goals
- Meet my budgeted profit for the year.
- Get high marks on the parent evaluations.

Marketing Plan

Program Benefits

1. I provide an individually designed learning program for each child to help the children learn and grow.

2. I offer planned events with two other providers in my neighborhood so the children can play and learn social skills with a variety of other children.

3. We are close to a public park that has many child-friendly activities (such as swing sets, a ball field, etc.) for the children to enjoy.

Child Care Resource and Referral (CCR&R) Updates

☑ I have updated my CCR&R in the last six months about my openings.
My last CCR&R update was on 1/1/2008

Market Rate Information Survey

	Infants	Toddlers	Preschoolers	Schoolagers
Home 1	$170	$155	$140	$110
Home 2	$165	$150	$135	$110
Home 3	$165	$150	$135	$105
Home 4	$160	$145	$130	$100
Home 5	$150	$135	$120	$95
Center 1	$190	$165	$150	$125
Center 2	$185	$160	$145	$125
Center 3	$175	$155	$145	$110

Marketing Activities

January	Update child care resource and referral about my program.
February	Hold a Valentine's Day party and invite children's parents.
March	Offer the parents a finder's fee for referring a new family.
April	Attend association meeting and ask other providers for marketing ideas.
May	Distribute 50 flyers to local businesses.
June	Update child care resource and referral about my program, and ask for marketing ideas.
July	Start a newsletter for my program.
August	Start a photo album that shows the benefits of my program
September	Ask at least two other providers who have a waiting list how they keep it full.
October	Pass out my business cards to trick-or-treaters.
November	Identify a new benefit to help promote my program.
December	Hold a holiday party and invite the families in my program and those on my waiting list.

Feedback

☑ I will ask my clients to complete a written evaluation this year in December.

I will collect feedback about my program this year from

☑ CCR&R (in June)
☑ Food Program sponsor (in March)
☑ Government subsidy program (in August)
☑ Child care licensor (in October)

Insurance Plan

Homeowners Insurance Policy

Insurance company Met Life   Policy # 709931
Insurance agent Jeff Williams   Phone # 555-222-1111

☑ I have written proof that my home is fully covered while I am operating a business in my home.

☑ I have written proof that my homeowners policy fully covers the contents of my home used in my business (my business property).

Vehicle Insurance Policy

Insurance company Farmer's Insurance   Policy # 00009363425
Insurance agent Melinda Lopez   Phone # 333-111-6666

☑ I have written proof that I am fully covered for all business uses of my vehicle, both when transporting children and on other business trips.

Business Liability Insurance Policy
Insurance company Duke Insurance   Policy # 409332
Insurance agent Dee Ellington   Phone # 555-000-8888

Disability Income Insurance Policy
Insurance company Duke Insurance   Policy # 4666222
Insurance agent Dee Ellington   Phone # 555-000-8888

Program Plan

Purpose or Mission Statement
I give all the children in my care a loving, child-centered environment that will help them grow to their full potential.

Program Choices
Goal for number of children in each age group:

	Full-time	Part-time
Infants	1	0
Toddlers	2	0
Preschoolers	4	0
Schoolagers	3	0

❏ Any rooms off-limits to children
❏ Any rooms used 100% for business
❏ Plan to hire any employees

Child Care Curriculum
☑ Self-designed curriculum

Professional Development Plan

My Background, Training, and Skills
I have one child of my own, age three. I have taken three semesters of early childhood education classes at Metro State University, and I expect to graduate in another two years.

Professional Development Goal for the Coming Year
Take three classes more than my state licensing requirements.

Professional Organizations
☑ Member of local family child care association
    Name of association: Minnesota Licensed Family Child Care Association
☑ Member of National Association for Family Child Care

Record-Keeping Plan

I will track the following information:

☑ each child's daily attendance: entered daily into the *Redleaf Calendar-Keeper*

☑ payments from parents: entered weekly into the *Redleaf Calendar-Keeper*

☑ Food Program reimbursements and claim forms: updated monthly and kept in my Food Program folder in my file cabinet

☑ business expenses (receipts, cancelled checks, credit or debit card statements): filed weekly in the folders in my file cabinet

☑ hours worked in my home: filed in my file cabinet; updated weekly

☑ business insurance policies: filed in my file cabinet; updated annually

☑ child care contracts: signed originals filed in my file cabinet; updated annually

☑ federal and state tax returns and quarterly estimated tax payments: filed in my file cabinet; updated quarterly

☑ monthly bank statements (business and personal accounts): filed in my file cabinet; updated monthly

☑ I have a separate business checking account.
Name of bank: Highland Bank

Financial Plan

See attached budget.

APPENDIX C

Financial Tools

Cash Flow Projection

	JAN 5	FEB 4	MAR 5	APR 4	MAY 4	JUN 5	JUL 4	AUG 4	SEP 5	OCT 4	NOV 4	DEC 5	Total
Number of weeks in month	5	4	5	4	4	5	4	4	5	4	4	5	
Income (cash inflows)													
Cash on hand	0	(1,070)	(680)	1,419	1,615	3,302	3,689	3,561	3,565	3,633	3,709	3,579	
Infant @ $175/week		700	875	700	700	0	0	0	875	720	720	900	6,190
Toddler @ $145/week	725	580	725	580	580	0	0	0	725	580	580	725	5,800
Toddler @ $145/week			725	580	580	725	580	435	725	580	580	725	6,235
Preschooler @ $125/week		500	625	500	500	625	500	375	625	500	500	625	5,875
Preschooler @ $125/week				500	500	625	500	375	625	500	500	625	4,750
Preschooler @ $125/week						625	500	375	625	500	500	625	3,750
Registration fees	50	25	25	25		25							150
Holding fees		45	109	182	182	182	182	149	112	281	225	225	1,874
Food Program reimbursements						200	200	200					600
Grant			500										500
Total	775	1,850	3,584	3,067	3,042	3,007	2,462	1,909	4,312	3,661	3,605	4,450	35,724
Expenses (cash outflows)													
Advertising	50	50	50			50			50				250
Vehicle expenses	25	25	40	50	60	60	70	60	70	40	40	40	580
Business liability insurance	375						375						750
Disability income insurance	350						350						700
Loan interest	30	30	30	30	30	30	30	30	30	30	30	30	360
Office expenses	40	40	40	40	40	40	40	40	40	40	40	40	480
Repairs		600									600		1,200
Children's supplies	80	80	80	80	80	80	80	80	80	80	80	80	960
Food	200	240	400	400	400	300	300	250	550	450	450	500	4,440
Toys	100	150	100	100				150	150	50	200		1,000
Household supplies	70	70	70	70	70	70	70	70	70	70	70	70	840
Field trips						50	50						100
Professional development	50			50			50	50	50	50	50		350
Property taxes				600						600			1,200
Mortgage payment	100	100	100	100	100	100	100	100	100	100	100	100	1,200
Utilities	75	75	75	75	75	75	75	75	75	75	75	75	900
Homeowners insurance				600									600
Repairs	200			100		50							350
Business property insurance	100												100
Estimated taxes				576		715			979				2,270
Retirement contribution												2,000	2,000
Total	1,845	1,460	985	2,871	855	1,620	1,590	905	2,244	1,585	1,735	2,935	20,630
Net profit (income − expenses)	(1,070)	390	2,599	196	2,187	1,387	872	1,004	2,068	2,076	1,870	1,515	15,094
Personal draw			500		500	1,000	1,000	1,000	2,000	2,000	2,000	2,000	12,000
Cash on hand (cash inflows − cash outflows)	(1,070)	(680)	1,419	1,615	3,302	3,689	3,561	3,565	3,633	3,709	3,579	3,094	

Sample Cash Flow Projection

The facing page shows a sample cash flow projection that Raina has created for the first year of her new family child care business. Her numbers reflect the following assumptions:

January   Raina's business liability and disability insurance premiums ($375 + 350 = $725) will be due in January, which will help create a loss in her first month in business.

February   Raina's first Food Program reimbursement check will arrive in February. (The delay involved in processing this check also contributes to her loss in January.)

March   Raina has applied for a $500 grant to buy some toys. If her application is approved, she'll receive the money in March and spend it in April. This month she also plans to take $500 as a personal draw to pay herself.

April   On April 15, Raina's first-quarter estimated taxes will be due (as well as the first half of her property tax). She projects that her first-quarter net profit will be $2,599 + $390 − $1,070 = $1,919. Since her family is in the 30% income tax bracket, she projects that she'll owe $1,919 x 30% = $576 in estimated taxes.

May   Raina will take another $500 draw this month.

June   Raina estimates that she will reach full enrollment by this month, so she plans to raise her draw to $1,000. On June 15, her estimated taxes for April and May will be due. She projects that her net profit for those two months will be $196 + $2,187 = $2,383, so she will owe $2,383 x 30% = $715. Also, two of the children will be gone for the summer, and she'll charge a holding fee of $100 a month instead of her normal rate from June through August. This will also mean lower food expenses and Food Program reimbursements over the summer.

July   Raina's business liability and disability insurance premiums ($725) will be due again in July.

August   Raina plans to take a one-week unpaid vacation in August, so she projects only three weeks of income this month and a lower Food Program check in September.

September On September 15, Raina's estimated taxes for June through August will be due. She projects that her net profit for those months will be $3,263, so she will owe $3,263 x 30% = $979. This month, she also plans to raise her rates for infant care by $5 a week (effective in October) and will increase her draw to $2,000.

October   The second half of Raina's property tax will be due on October 15.

November   Raina plans to set aside $800 this month to repaint the children's play room, repair any broken toys, and replace any other damaged items.

December   Raina will contribute $2,000 to her retirement savings account.

Blank Budget Form

Income

Income from parents

     Infants $_____/week x _____ weeks x _____ children $_____

     Toddlers $_____/week x _____ weeks x _____ children $_____

     Preschoolers $_____/week x _____ weeks x _____ children $_____

       Total $_____

Program fees

     Registration fees $_____ per child x _____ children $_____

Food Program income[a]

     $_____ per child per day x 5 days/week

     x _____weeks x _____ children $_____

Gross income $_____

Income reductions[b]

     Partial enrollment reduction (20%) $_____

     State subsidy program clients (5%) $_____

     Missed payments (2%) $_____

     Provider sick days (2%) $_____

       Total $_____

Net income $_____

Expenses

Business supplies

       Children's supplies $_____

       Food $_____

       Toys $_____

       Household supplies $_____

       Other supplies (such as for special field trips) $_____

       Total $_____

Other business expenses

       Professional development $_____

       Advertising $_____

       Vehicle[c] $_____

       Depreciation of household items (furniture, appliances, etc.) $_____

       Business liability insurance $_____

       Office expenses $_____

       Repairs of toys, furniture, and equipment $_____

       Total $_____

Home expenses[d]

       Property tax $_____

       Mortgage interest $_____

       Utilities $_____

       Home repairs $_____

       Homeowners insurance $_____

       Business property insurance $_____

       Home depreciation or rent $_____

       Total $_____

Blank Budget Form *(continued)*

Business loan (for start-up expenses)			
Repayment of principal	$_____		
Loan interest	$_____		
Total		$_____	
Other expenses			
Employees	$_____		
Total		$_____	
Total expenses			$_____
Net profit before taxes and retirement contribution[e] (net income – total expenses)			$_____
Retirement contribution		$_____	
Net profit after retirement contribution[f]			$_____
Taxes			
Social Security taxes[g]		$_____	
Federal income taxes[h]		$_____	
State income taxes[i]		$_____	
Total		$_____	
Net profit after taxes (net profit before retirement – total taxes)			$_____
Cash on hand at the end of the year (net profit after taxes – retirement contribution)			$_____

a. Project your reimbursements for the upcoming year based on the current rate that applies to your program.

b. Because these reductions are percentages of gross income, note that they reduce both parent fees and Food Program income.

c. For this number, multiply your business mileage by the current IRS mileage reimbursement rate.

d. For the numbers in this section, multiply your actual home expenses by your Time-Space percentage. If you aren't sure what your Time-Space percentage will be, you can use 40% as a ballpark estimate.

e. Use this number to calculate your Social Security taxes.

f. Use this number to calculate your income taxes.

g. If your net profit before taxes is greater than $400, enter 15.3% of that total on this line; otherwise, enter 0.

h. Consult a tax professional for the amount that you should budget for federal income tax.

i. Consult a tax professional for the amount that you should budget for state income tax.